Spookiest Objects

Terrance Zepke

Copyright © 2017 by Terrance Zepke

Safari Publishing

All queries should be directed to www.safaripublishing.net.

For more about this author, visit www.terrancezepke.com.

Library of Congress Cataloging-in-Publication Data

Zepke, Terrance

Spookiest Objects: Discover the World's Most Haunted Objects / Terrance Zepke p. cm.

ISBN: 978-1-942738-21-3

1. Cursed Objects. 2. Haunted Objects. 3. Paranormal Phenomenon. 4. Hauntings-America. 5. Hauntings-World. I. Title.

First edition

10 9 8 7 6 5 4 3 2 1

SPOOKIEST OBJECTS:
DISCOVER THE WORLD'S MOST
HAUNTED OBJECTS

TERRANCE ZEPKE

Safari Publishing

See the back of this book for more spooky fun titles by this author and a sneak peak of A GHOST HUNTER'S GUIDE TO THE MOST HAUNTED PLACES IN AMERICA.

CONTENTS

About the Author

Terrance Zepke loves ghost stories and travel. She has lived and traveled all over the world during her career as a travel writer. She has traveled to every continent and had all kinds of adventures—from dog-sledding in the Arctic to an overnight ghost investigation in a creepy lunatic asylum. Even though she has lived in many great places, such as Honolulu and London, she calls the Carolinas home and swears she will never live anywhere else. She can't decide which state she likes best, so she divides her time between North and South Carolina. She grew up in the South Carolina Lowcountry, which is what ignited her interest in ghosts. The Lowcountry is full of haunted places and tales of boo hags, hoodoo, and haints. North Carolina's Outer Banks' history is full of pirates, lighthouses, and shipwrecks. Terrance has written numerous books on these subjects, as well as many travel guides, including her popular *Terrance Talks Travel* series. See the back of this book for a complete list of her titles.

Introduction

The thing about haunted places is that it is nearly impossible to say with absolute certainty that a place is haunted. You can document all kinds of incidents and encounters, which support the theory that a place is haunted. One can argue that there is no rational explanation for the things that have occurred, but that doesn't mean that paranormal activity can be proven definitively. It is nearly impossible to prove without doubt ghostly activity because noises can be explained away and sightings can be dismissed by skeptics, even when caught on film.

When you're talking about haunted objects, it gets all the more difficult to link a haunting to a particular object. How can you say for sure that an illness or death or any other fate is linked to a particular object? The very notion is contradictory to logic, but the supernatural is all about defying logic. The definition of supernatural is "a manifestation or event attributed to some force beyond scientific understanding or the laws of nature; a supernatural being."

It is important to make the distinction that an object is not *haunted*, although that is how these objects are often described as there seems to be no better way to put it. However, objects are *possessed* by a spirit, which is usually an evil entity. This may sound like semantics but it is a critical distinction because an inanimate object cannot be haunted, but it can be possessed or inhabited by a spirit. That is why I have described them as "spookiest" objects.

I don't want to delve too deep into this discussion because this is not my area of expertise. That said, a bit of explaining must be done so that this makes sense to readers. I have done some research on the subject, and I attended a fascinating lecture about haunted objects given by a renowned expert, John Zaffis. Zaffis starred in the SyFy show, *Haunted Collector*, and runs the Paranormal and Demonology Research Society of New England, which he founded in 1998. He is the director of the Museum of the Paranormal in Stratford, Connecticut.

During this enlightening seminar, Zaffis revealed that people innocently bring home souvenirs and buy thrift store items that have spirit attachments which make the object seem like it is cursed or haunted. He shared how he once helped a woman who brought a mask home with her from the Caribbean. As soon as she brought it into her home, all these terrible things began happening. She assumed that a curse had been placed on the mask. She didn't realize that an evil spirit can attach itself to an object and then manifest itself onto the object's owners or anyone else who comes into contact with the object. Zaffis has helped many others who discovered they had unwittingly brought home toys, dolls, furniture, jewelry, and antiques that were possessed with demonic forces or "residues of the dead," according to Zaffis.

It is terrifying to think we could bring evil into our homes by bringing home a piece of furniture or a toy. But it happens every day, I imagine. This book is full of such stories. You will read about Annabelle, a Raggedy Ann doll that is one of the most disturbing stories in this entire book. There are also tales about haunted jewelry, paintings, and furnishings that will make your toes curl. In fact, every object in this book has wreaked havoc on the owners of the items. Some of the *places* where these objects ended up are also considered to be among the most haunted in America, such as Belcourt Castle (Royal Chairs of Belcourt), Baleroy Mansion (Amanda's Chair), and Myrtles Plantation (Myrtles Mirror).

I have written dozens of ghost books, but this one was the most intriguing to me because it delved into an aspect of the paranormal that I have not addressed previously. It seems inconceivable that so much tragedy and darkness can be connected to these objects, but once you wrap your mind around the idea that these objects are haunted (inhabited) by evil spirits, it makes sense, at least as much as something like this can. And after you read about Robert the Doll, The Conjure Chest, Busby's Death Chair, and all the other haunted objects discussed in this reference, you will surely realize or at least suspect something scary and supernatural happening.

One of my favorite things about writing ghost books is researching them. This is fairly straightforward when it comes to places, such as old plantations and asylums because there is so much documentation in the way of history and paranormal investigations. However, it was problematic to get a complete and accurate account for these objects because some of the origins are unknown, witnesses are deceased or their whereabouts unknown, and some of the objects were destroyed or hidden long ago. Often, accounts provide different names or spellings of names, dates and times, and histories. In a couple of cases, such as the Basano Vase, I had precious few facts to go on. However, I have done my best to create the most accurate composite of truths based on the information available.

I think the important thing to remember is that despite any discrepancies, it is obvious that something strange sinister and supernatural is happening with these objects. For example, inanimate objects do not move on their own, but witnesses have seen Anna's Wedding Dress and Anabelle the Doll do so. What logical explanation can there possibly be for what has been seen in the Myrtles Mirror? If any part of the family's claims about *The Crying Boy* is true, then how can you not believe that a spirit must be involved?

As I have pointed out, it is hard to make a definitive connection between these objects and all the deaths and devastation that have occurred to those associated with them. But all these incidents cannot be coincidence, and no other 'earthly' explanation seems plausible. But even if you choose not to believe that objects can be haunted, I believe you will still enjoy reading these spooky stories.

So read on to learn more about this list I have compiled of the most haunted objects in the world and draw your own conclusions.

Author's Note: I hope you like reading this book as much as I enjoyed researching and writing it. This is the fourth book in my *SPOOKIEST* series. You will find a complete list of book titles at the end of this reference. There will only be one more book in this series, but I promise you that I will keep writing ghost books—and chasing ghosts!

For more information on other books that I have written and to check out my ghost gallery, to sign up for my **MOSTLY GHOSTLY** blog, and to receive free ghost reports, visit www.terrancezepke.com.

Haunted Houses

All houses wherein men have lived and died
Are haunted houses. Through the open doors
The harmless phantoms on their errands glide,
With feet that make no sound upon the floors.

We meet them at the door-way, on the stair,
Along the passages they come and go,
Impalpable impressions on the air,
A sense of something moving to and fro.

There are more guests at the table than the hosts
Invited; the illuminated hall
Is thronged with quiet, inoffensive ghosts,
As silent as the pictures on the wall.

The stranger at my fireside cannot see
The forms I see, nor hear the sounds I hear;
He but perceives what is; while unto me
All that has been is visible and clear.

We have no title-deeds to house or lands
Owners and occupants of earlier dates
From graves forgotten stretch their dusty hands,
And hold in mortmain still their old estates.

The spirit-world around this world of sense
Floats like an atmosphere, and everywhere
Wafts through these earthly mists and vapours dense
A vital breath of more ethereal air.

Our little lives are kept in equipoise
By opposite attractions and desires;
The struggle of the instinct that enjoys,
And the more noble instinct that aspires.

These perturbations, this perpetual jar
Of earthly wants and aspirations high,
Come from the influence of an unseen star
An undiscovered planet in our sky.

And as the moon from some dark gate of cloud
Throws o'er the sea a floating bridge of light,
Across whose trembling planks our fancies crowd
Into the realm of mystery and night,

So from the world of spirits there descends
A bridge of light, connecting it with this,
O'er whose unsteady floor, that sways and bends,
Wander our thoughts above the dark abyss.

-Henry Wadsworth Longfellow (1807 – 1882)

Amanda's Chair

Location: Philadelphia, Pennsylvania

Origin: Circa 1817

Visitor Information: 111W. Mermaid Lane. This is a private residence and is not open to the public.

About The Haunted Object: Let's start first with the house, which is reportedly haunted. The Baleroy Mansion, named after Balleroy in France, is a thirty-two-room estate situated on 22,088-feet of land in one of the most affluent neighborhoods in Philadelphia, Chestnut Hill. The house has roughly 6,000-square feet of living space and includes a large carriage house. It was built in 1911 by a carpenter who allegedly murdered his wife in this very house. It was bought by the Easby family in 1926. The house stayed in the family until 2005.

Family members all claim to have experienced some paranormal phenomena. This ranged from hallucinations to ghost sightings. Family and visitors have seen an old woman dressed in black with a cane. She hovers in a corner on the second floor of the house. There has been unexplainable knocking and banging.

A painting once came off the wall and landed more than fifteen feet away from where it hung. A closer inspection revealed the nail was still firmly embedded in the wall and there was nothing wrong with the picture wire on the back of the painting. There didn't seem to be any logical explanation as to why it fell or how it came to land so far from the wall where it had been mounted.

A few folks believe they have seen the ghost of Thomas Jefferson in the dining room near a grandfather clock that may have once belonged to him. Some of the antiques in the house have been gifts or heirlooms from famous people, such as Thomas Jefferson, Napoleon Bonaparte, and General George Meade, who was George Meade Easby's great grandfather. He was also a Civil War hero.

Another lingering spirit is Steven Easby. He died in childhood in this house. A little blond-haired boy has been seen looking out the window. An uncle and George Meade Easby's mother also haunts the house. George claims his mother's spirit helped him on many occasions. Once, she lured him to an old desk where he found important papers. Another time, she showed him where some valuable candlesticks had been hidden in the attic.

George once awoke in the middle of the night when he felt someone grab his arm. He quickly turned on the lamp to see who it was, only to discover there was no one in the room! George had grown accustomed to strange goings-on. The alarm system often tripped on for no good reason. The electricity goes off for no obvious reason. It could just be old wiring, but the Easby family didn't think so.

A psychic once came to the house to investigate. As soon as Judith Haimes entered, she exclaimed: "*My God, I can't believe how many spirits are in this house!*" The house has been featured on several paranormal television shows and books because it is considered one of the most haunted houses in America.

George Gordon Meade Easby (June 3, 1918 – December 11, 2005) lived in Baleroy all his life—and may still be there, at least in spirit. He was a man with many interests. His occupation is listed as an artist, actor, antique collector, author, radio host, political commentator, producer, and philanthropist. He also worked for the U.S. State Department for many years.

George Meade Easby was the last of the Easby family to live in Baleroy. He found a note in his father's old desk that read *"I was not brought up to believe in ghosts and to trust only what science could explain, however, I have seen the ghosts, and there is no reason to be afraid."* George died in 2005. His spirit may still be at Baleroy. He once told a reporter he would probably haunt the place if the future owners didn't take good care of it. But he may have hung around anyway. George loved Baleroy and always took comfort in its many lingering spirits, except for one known as Amanda.

Amanda is an evil entity that came to Baleroy at some point and won't leave. She often yanks doors open and slams them shut violently. She takes on the appearance of a weird red mist. She does her best to lure you into the Blue Room and into a certain chair, which has become known as Amanda's chair. The chair is an ugly 200-year-old blue upholstered wingback chair that reportedly once belonged to Napoleon Bonaparte. The Blue Room is an eighteenth-century drawing room which contains an assortment of antiques and secret compartments.

Amanda has tricked at least four people into sitting in this death chair. This includes two housekeepers, George's cousin, and Paul Kimmons, who was the Baleroy curator and a close friend of George's. He witnessed Amanda (or rather the ectoplasmic red mist known as Amanda) floating down the stairway one day. After that, he began seeing her everywhere. Later that week, he felt compelled to sit in the wing-backed chair. He had never done so before, but now he felt he needed to do so. Within a few weeks, he was dead. A housekeeper died while in the seat. She just slumped over and took her last breath.

After that, a tape was placed across the chair from arm to arm to prevent anyone from sitting down. I have been unable to find out who has possession of this chair. The house was robbed in 1992. It is estimated that more than $200,000 in antiques were stolen. The chair may have been among those items.

Or it may have been sold by Robert Paul Yriguyen, who was entrusted with Easby's financial affairs and personal care in 2005. It is believed that during the next few years he sold more than 100,000 antiques and handled millions of dollars in the Easby estate.

Or the chair may have been sold or donated in 2012 when the house was sold. All remaining antiques, furnishings and antique cars were sold or donated to museums at that time. This includes a 1954 Rolls-Royce Silver Wraith, which once belonged to Prince Aly Khan, who was actress Rita Hayworth's husband. Speaking of cars, phantom vehicles have been heard many times over the years. The roar of a motor from an old or antique car racing up the driveway has often been heard, but no vehicle was found in the driveway.

Anna's Wedding Dress

Location: Altoona, Pennsylvania

Origin: Circa mid-1800s

Visitor Information: The Baker Mansion Museum is OPEN TO THE PUBLIC for tours by appointment and special events. 3419 Oak Lane, Altoona, PA 16602. http://www.blairhistory.org/. A virtual tour can be taken at http://www.blairhistory.org/baker-mansion.html.

About The Haunted Object: It's a story that's as old as time. A young girl falls in love with a boy—the wrong boy. In this case, the girl is Anna Baker, who is the youngest daughter of Elias Baker, a wealthy businessman.

Elias and a partner bought a small furnace company and grew it into a hugely, profitable business. Elias bought out his partner in 1844 and worked hard to make the company bigger and more profitable. The self-made man finally had the money to build his dream house.

In 1849, he hired Robert Cary Long Jr., who was considered one of the best in the area, which is what Elias Baker wanted. He spared no expense for the architect or his new home. Long designed a grand house for Elias Baker. It was a Greek-Revival style mansion complete with black walnut woodwork, Italian marble fireplaces, and exquisite furniture imported from Belgium.

Despite his humble beginnings, Elias was a snob. He wanted only the best for himself and his family. He expected his daughter to marry well. Elias had worked hard to secure his family's place in society and he expected his extended family to reflect that prominence.

As was the custom in those days, his daughter had a hope chest. A hope chest was a young woman's accumulation of clothes and domestic furnishings (such as silver and linen) kept in anticipation of her marriage. Anna and her mother carefully collected the items she would need when she got married. Anna already had her most important item— her wedding dress. It was a one-of-a-kind floor length, hand-sewn gown featuring exquisite lace and mother-of-pearl buttons. It was enchanting. She often pulled it out of the trunk and held it up in front of her while looking in the mirror. Sometimes she went so far as to put the dress on and twirled around enough so that the hem swirled and floated in the air. She was going to be a beautiful bride, she mused as she studied her reflection. It was going to be the happiest day of her life. She pictured her perfect wedding to her perfect husband while wearing her perfect dress.

But it was more than a dream. Anna had a secret. She had already found her husband-to-be. She began pulling her dress out more often and envisioning her wedding day more and more. She couldn't believe how lucky she was. She was so happy, except that she worried how her father would handle the news. Her betrothed was a steel worker, so she knew her father wouldn't approve. It would take time and all her powers of persuasion to win him over.

The couple met secretly, due to that fact. As things grew serious between the two, the young man pushed Anna to tell Elias about their relationship. He was in love and didn't care who knew it. Anna was in love, but wasn't in a hurry to confront her father. The more she thought about it, the more anxious she became about his reaction.

The impatient young man persisted and finally Anna relented. They agreed he would come to her house the next evening and introduce himself to her father. Anna was so nervous she barely slept a wink and could hardly eat a thing due to the butterflies in her stomach. As the appointed time drew closer, it was all she could do to keep from pacing the floor. She kept glancing out the window until she saw him coming up the porch steps. Her heart nearly fluttered out of her chest as her father opened the door and she heard the exchange.

It was worse than she had expected. After introducing himself and explaining the reason for his visit, Anna's father began yelling at the young man. By some accounts, the poor fellow never made it through the front door. He was never permitted to come inside and make a case for himself. He was told to leave, and that he did not have permission to see Anna again—and then he slammed the door before the young man could respond.

Anna ran across the room and to stop him from leaving, but her father stopped her. He gently pushed her away from the door and told her how disappointed he was with her. After everything he had done to guarantee Anna's place in society, she paid him back by carrying on with a lowly factory worker? Anna tried to reason with him, but Elias refused to listen. He ordered her to go to her room.

Anna and her boyfriend hoped Elias would calm down and come around, but he didn't. Instead, he grew angrier the more he thought about it. He had the young man fired from his job and saw to it that no one else in town would hire him. The penniless, unemployed young man had no choice but to leave town. He wasn't even permitted to say goodbye to Anna.

Anna was devastated. When she looked at her hope chest, especially her wedding dress, all she saw now was dashed dreams. The lovely gown represented everything she had lost—the love of her life, her perfect wedding, and happily ever after. She asked her mother to get rid of it. Her mother tried to talk her daughter out of it, explaining that when she found the right boy, she would want the dress. Her words fell on deaf ears. Anna swore she would never love again or get married.

Hetty didn't know what to do. She hated seeing her daughter so miserable. She tried to intervene but her husband had the final word, so there was little she could do. She was unable to change his mind or do anything to help her daughter except to get rid of the dress. It was all that Anna had asked and the least she could do.

Elizabeth Bell, a peer of Anna's, ended up with the dress. This was unfortunate because the two girls had never gotten along. There had always been a rivalry between them. When Elizabeth got married wearing Anna's wedding dress, it was the final straw for Anna. She was crushed and what was left of her fragile heart was shattered.

Anna died in 1914, many believe of a broken heart. She had lost her will to live after her father ran her husband-to-be out of town. She never married. And she never forgave her father for what he had done.

The dress was given to the historical society, which put it on exhibit in the Baker Mansion Museum. It was kept in a glass display case and believed to be haunted by Anna's spirit, as is the Baker house.

Visitors and staff of the historical society claim to have seen the ghosts of Anna, Elias, and Hetty. Anna is usually seen in the parlor and her old bedroom. Elias is seen in the dining room, and Hetty is seen on occasion on the stairs. All these spirits disappear almost as quickly as they appear. Banging is heard most often as if a cane is repeatedly hitting the floor. Also, unexplainable odors, cold spots, furniture being moved, and footsteps have been reported too. There is a music box that begins playing and a security alarm that often goes off for no good reason.

The house is open to visitors, but the dress has been removed from public display. Reportedly, the dress "danced" on its own. The dress moved so forcefully that it rocked the display case. It often appeared as if it would topple the case over to the ground or shatter the glass. How could an inanimate object secured in a case where no wind, draft, or fan could propel it move in such a fierce fashion? Has Anna's spirit attached itself to the dress? Perhaps her angry spirit is unable to stop dreaming about the life she never got to have?

No one has found a better explanation. The museum staff were so perplexed and frightened whenever these incidents occurred that it led to the decision to remove the dress from display, even though they have never publicly admitted that is the reason it was removed. Their reasons don't make any sense. They claim the dress is discoloring as a result of being displayed, but how can that be true when the dress is kept out of the sun in a climate-controlled room in a special display case? As preposterous as it sounds, the explanation that Anna's spirit has reclaimed her long lost dress makes more sense.

According to an anonymous source, the historical society conducted clandestine investigations to try to determine how the dress can move in an airtight, secure case. They installed hidden cameras, convinced they would discover it was a prank or some other perfectly reasonable explanation, but the cameras only revealed that no one (at least no one human) was in the room when the activity occurred. They could find no logical explanation for these events. That leaves only a supernatural explanation…

AnnaBELLE

Annabelle

Ed and Lorraine Warren with Annabelle

Location: Warren's Occult Museum (Monroe, Connecticut)

Origin: Unknown before the doll was purchased in a thrift store in 1970.

Visitor Information: Warren's Occult Museum is currently closed to the public due to zoning issues. Please visit their website for updates.

http://www.warrens.net/Occult-Museum-Tours.html

About The Haunted Object: This story began in 1970. A college student named Donna received a vintage Raggedy Ann-looking doll from her mother, who found the doll in a thrift store. Donna took the doll, which she named Annabelle, back to her apartment. That's when the nightmare began.

Donna and her roommate, Angie, became convinced the doll was moving. At first, they thought they were mistaken, but after they made a point of noting the doll's location before leaving the apartment each morning for school, and then discovering it in another room upon their return, they knew there was something seriously weird going on. And not only was the doll repeatedly found in new locations; it was found in different positions, as well. Sometimes, the doll would be in a sitting position, and other times it was "standing" on its legs beside the dining room table. This was a seemingly impossible position given the anatomy of the doll. Sometimes, they returned to find the doll sitting with its arms folded in a most unnatural way. It got so the doll was never where Donna left it. Once, they deliberately placed the doll on the couch before leaving for class and returned home to find it on Donna's bed—and the door to the bedroom was closed, which Donna distinctly remembered leaving open.

They also found notes on pieces of paper that resembled parchment. These scraps of paper had only a few words scribbled on them, such as "*Help us*" and *Help Lou*." One night Donna found a substance on the doll's hand that looked like blood.

The nursing students weren't the only ones spooked. Their good friend, Lou, was also creeped out. He began having nightmares about the doll attacking him. One night when Lou and the girls were in the living room hanging out, they heard noises coming from Donna's bedroom. It sounded like someone was moving around the room. Cautiously, Lou approached the bedroom. He threw open the door and looked inside without entering the room. He saw nothing out of the ordinary. Bravely, he crept into the room and peered into every nook and cranny. He didn't see anything amiss, but he felt a strange sensation.

He spun around and saw Annabelle in the corner, but he had seen her on the bed when he first entered the room! The strange sensation changed to a burning pain in his chest. As he clutched his chest, he felt claw marks. Looking down his shirt, he saw seven huge, ugly claw marks across his chest. They looked awful. Donna thought he should go to the emergency room, but Lou didn't want to because he didn't know how to explain what had happened. The sinister wounds were mysteriously gone the next day. How could such vicious injuries just disappear? It made no sense at all, but he knew that Annabelle was responsible.

Not knowing what to do and badly scared, they contacted a medium. What the psychic revealed was shocking and disturbing. She told them that the body of a seven-year-old girl named Annabelle Higgin was found in the field where their apartment building now stood. Her murder was never solved. The psychic believed that the spirit of the deceased child had attached itself to the doll. Donna and Angie thought perhaps the spirit was just looking for peace, so they gave the spirit permission to stay.

This was the worst thing they could do because they had unwittingly invited the spirit into their home. They may have felt they were compassionate, but what was only going to lead to more problems, as they soon found out.

The incidents escalated, and they found themselves stressed out and scared and unable to sleep. They dreaded coming home. The final straw was when an unseen presence nearly strangled Lou one evening. At their wit's end, Angie and Donna contacted a priest and told him their story. The shrewd priest, Father Hegan, got in touch with another priest, Father Cooke, who was more knowledgeable in the area of demonic possessions and exorcisms.

Father Cooke, in turn, contacted Ed and Lorraine Warren. Lorraine Warren is a gifted psychic, and Ed Warren is a respected demonologist.

The couple accompanied the Episcopalian priest to the girls' apartment. After studying the doll and speaking with the girls, the Warrens realized a demonic spirit was trying to possess a human host. The priest performed an exorcism. It had used the doll to gain entry into their lives and was in the process of taking possession of one of them.

This was one of the worst demonic hauntings they had encountered. The Warrens were confident that within another week or two the spirit would have harmed or even killed Donna, Angie, and Lou. After the lengthy exorcism procedure, the priest left. The Warrens also left with the doll. On their way home, they nearly wrecked several times as an unseen presence seemed to take control of the vehicle. Ed struggled to keep control of the car, and the couple doused the doll with holy water. After that, there was no more trouble controlling the vehicle.

Upon arriving home, Ed brought the doll into the house and sat it on his desk. As he sat down, he noticed the doll was levitating. This happened several times before the doll fell and did not levitate again. In the next couple of weeks, however, the doll began moving around their home. They called their priest, Father Bradford, to come and exorcise their home. Believing it was foolishness but willing to indulge his parishioners, Father Bradford promptly arrived.

When shown the doll, he said: *"You're just a doll, Annabelle, You can't hurt anyone."* He insisted on taking the doll with him. He was involved in a nearly fatal accident on his way home. Inexplicably, his brakes failed at a busy intersection.

The Warrens had a special case built to secure Annabelle. The case has never been opened, and the doll has never harmed anyone else. However, there is an interesting event that occurred. A couple came to visit the Warrens' Occult Museum. After hearing Ed explain the story of Annabelle, the young man reacted strangely. Obviously doubting the doll could do any harm, he banged on the case and challenged the evil spirit to come and get him.

Shocked and frightened by the man's actions, Ed asked him to leave immediately. He warned him that he didn't know what he was doing, that it was not wise to provoke an evil spirit. Laughing, the young man and his girlfriend raced up the road on his motorcycle. Within a few miles, he lost control of the bike and crashed into a tree. He died instantly, but the girl lived. She was badly injured and spent a year recovering from her injuries.

FYI: Ed and Lorraine Warren were well-known and controversial paranormal investigators. Ed was a self-taught and self-professed demonologist (who died in 2006), while Lorraine is a clairvoyant and psychic (who is still alive but in her 90s). Although controversial due to their field, the Warrens are considered pioneers and experts in paranormal research. They founded the New England Society for Psychic Research in 1952. It is the oldest ghost investigating group in New England. The Warrens have participated in more than 10,000 paranormal cases. They have given hundreds of lectures and written several books, including *Ghost Hunters: True Stories From the World's Most Famous Demonologists.* They have been featured in *Paranormal State, A Haunting*, and *Scariest Places on Earth.* Some of their real-life cases have led to movies, such as *Amityville Horror, Annabelle*, and *The Conjuring.* www.warrens.net.

Warren's Occult Museum

The Warren's Occult Museum is the oldest and only museum of its kind. This world-renowned museum has attracted hundreds of thousands of visitors from across the world. The museum houses the largest collection of haunted objects, many of which are kept under lock and key. Check the website for updates on the museum reopening at www.warrens.net/Occult-Museum-Tours.html

Basano Vase

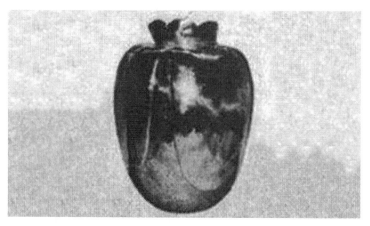

This is one of the few images of the Basano Vase.

Location: Unknown

Origin: Unknown

Visitor Information: None

About The Haunted Object: According to legend, a bride received this vase as a wedding gift in the 15th century. She took possession of it on her wedding night and was later found dead that same night, clutching the vase in her hand. One account reports she died of "mysterious circumstances" while another claims she was murdered.

As the vase made its way through the family, all those who came into possession of it died untimely deaths. Eventually, the family came to believe they possessed a haunted object. They boxed up the vase and put it into storage. According to the family, a note had been enclosed inside the box containing the vase that read *"Beware. This vase brings death."* It was written by the family member who had hidden the vase to warn anyone who might discover the hidden vase one day. No more incidents occurred until 1988.

This was when the vase resurfaced. It was sold at auction for $2,500. When the vase was auctioned off, there was no warning note in the box. Had it somehow gotten separated from the vase during handling? Had the family member who wanted rid of the cursed vase removed it? Had the auction company decided it should be disposed of if they were going to be able to sell the item? After all, such an ominous note would be discouraging to most buyers.

Unaware of the backstory of the vase, the new owner happily took possession of it. He proudly displayed it for three months, until his unexpected death. Once again, the vase was sold, and once again, the new owner soon died mysteriously. The vase kept changing hands with buyers including a surgeon, a pharmacist, an archeologist, and an unknown buyer. They each suffered untimely deaths soon after acquiring the vase.

The vicious cycle of death finally ceased one day when an owner threw the object out his window. A passing policeman was nearly struck by the falling object. Miraculously, the officer looked up and caught the vase just before it would have conked him squarely on the head. He marched up to the door of the house and banged on the front door.

He held the vase out to the occupant, angrily demanding an

explanation. The man apologized but backed away from the vase, throwing his hands up to show he didn't want the object back. In a rambling manner, he explained his belief that the vase was cursed and he wanted nothing to do with it. He had thrown it out the window in desperation, hoping it would shatter and be destroyed, thereby ending the curse.

The policeman noted the man seemed genuinely frightened and extremely agitated. Nonetheless, his story sounded like utter nonsense. There was no such thing as a cursed or haunted object; he told the man. Again he tried to return the vase. Mumbling an apology, the man quickly shut the door, leaving the policeman and the vase on his doorstep.

Taken aback, the cop started to knock on the door to confront the man about his behavior but decided not to spend any more time on this silly matter. If the man didn't want the vase, there was no crime. The policeman took the vase back to the station and told her superiors this strange story. The chief of police, who was a superstitious man, had heard stories about a haunted vase. He didn't want anything to do with the vase. He wanted it out of his police station as soon as possible. He told the policeman to take it down to the local museum and donate it to them on behalf of the police department.

The police officer went straight away to the museum with the vase. To her surprise, the museum refused to take the donation! They too had heard the stories of the cursed vase and didn't want any part of it. The curator had heard enough stories about cursed objects in his lifetime to be a believer. He kindly thanked the officer and the police department for their generous offer but suggested they find another "home" for the vase.

According to legend, the policy ultimately buried the vase in an undisclosed location. It is unknown whether they included a warning note, in case the vase was discovered one day. No more incidents have been reported, so I can only conclude that no one has unearthed the vase yet. It seems that all's well that ends well, at least until someone else takes possession of the cursed Basano Vase.

Busby's Death Chair

Location: Thirsk, North Yorkshire

Origin: 1669

Visitor Information: The chair is on display in the Thirsk Museum, which is OPEN TO THE PUBLIC from Easter to mid-November. 1416 Kirkgate, Thirsk, North Yorkshire, England Y07 1PQ.

www.thirskmuseum.org

About The Haunted Object: This story begins with Thomas Busby, who was a petty criminal with a quick temper. One evening, he got into an argument with his father-in-law, Daniel Awety. Unfortunately, Awety also had a bad temper. Their argument escalated, and threats were exchanged.

The next day, Daniel Awety's body was found in the woods near his home. He had been bludgeoned to death (Note: one account claims he was strangled). The police soon linked Busby to the murder and arrested him. A jury came to the same conclusion as the authorities and sentenced Busby to death by hanging.

On the way to the gallows, Busby was permitted a final request. He was allowed to have a final drink at his favorite pub. Busby had spent many evenings in this establishment enjoying pint after pint. Some nights he had as many as five or six pints of ale before stumbling home. Today, however, he only had time for one. It would be the last time he would enjoy his favorite ale sitting in his favorite chair in his favorite tavern. Since the gallows were just outside the pub, the guards didn't see the harm in indulging the man a dying wish.

As the guards signaled it was time to go, Busby stood up angrily and announced, *"Death shall come swiftly to anyone that dares to sit in my chair."* He pointed to the chair that he had knocked over as he abruptly stood to leave. He was executed on the stoop of his beloved pub in 1702.

Over the years, there have been dozens of documented deaths that are believed to be related to Busby's curse. The first was a tired chimney sweeper who sat in the chair to rest for a few minutes. He fell off the roof to his death shortly after getting out of the chair and returning to work.

During World War II, airmen stationed nearby frequented the tavern. Some thought the story about the cursed chair was pure rubbish and laughingly sat in the chair, telling Busby to come and get them. None of the men who sat in that chair returned from the war. They were all killed in action.

Many more deaths followed for those who dared to sit in the chair, including a young man who suffered a heart attack, a hitchhiker who was run over, and a motorcyclist who lost control of his bike and was killed.

In 1967, two Royal Air Force pilots crashed their vehicle on their way back to the base after taking turns sitting in the cursed chair. Both were killed upon impact.

After this incident, it was impossible for the tavern owner to ignore the link between the chair and all these deaths. Some may have been bad luck or such, but all these deaths so soon after sitting in the chair was impossible to dismiss. There was something evil about the object, he decided. The chair was removed from the tavern and stored in the basement.

There were no further tragic incidents until a workman came across the chair while in the basement. The workman didn't see the harm in resting for a bit, so he pulled the chair out of the corner and sat down. After resting for a few minutes, he got up and resumed his work. He died later that day. A roofer who also found the chair and sat in it while on break, fell to his death within minutes of getting out of the chair. A cleaning lady tripped over a box on the floor and fell into the chair. She soon died of a brain aneurysm. A delivery man unloaded some boxes in the basement. It had been a long, hard day. Spying the chair against the wall in the corner, he gratefully took a seat and had a short nap. An hour later, he crashed his delivery van and was pronounced dead by the time he arrived at the hospital.

Knowing something had to be done, but unsure what to do, the tavern owner gave the matter some serious thought. He could not give the chair away because that wouldn't solve the problem. People would continue to sit it and subsequently die. Storing the chair hadn't worked. He was afraid to destroy it. If anyone who sat in it was cursed, what would happen to the person who was responsible for destroying it? He wasn't about to find out! Finally, the solution came to him. He made a phone call and got the response he wanted.

In 1972, the Cursed Chair (also known as Busby's Death Chair) was donated to the Thirsk Museum. It is on display, but no one can sit in it accidentally or on purpose because it is hanging high on a wall in the museum's cottage kitchen. No one is allowed to even touch it, just to be on the safe side.

Outside the old inn, the old gallows where Busby was hanged can still be seen. The ghost of Thomas Busby has been seen near these gallows and inside the building. How do we know it's the ghost of Busby? It has a rope around its neck and a lolling head!

The World of James Herriot is across from the Thirsk Museum. It is the winner of the best small attraction in England. It features the life and books of author James Herriot.
http://www.worldofjamesherriot.com/

The legendary and haunted Busby Stoop Inn is now Jaipur Spice, an Indian restaurant. Busby Stoop Road, Thirsk. North Yorkshire, Y07 4EQ.

The hanging gallows are just outside the old tavern, which is now an Indian restaurant.

Conjure Chest

Location: Thomas D. Clark Center for Kentucky History

Origin: Circa 1850

Visitor Information: The museum is OPEN TO THE PUBLIC from Tuesday – Saturday, 10 a.m. – 5 p.m. $. 100 W. Broadway. Frankfort, Kentucky 40601. http://history.ky.gov/history-campus/

About The Haunted Object: Jacob Cooley was an affluent plantation owner, but he was a miserly man. He was always trying to get the best of anyone he did business with, and he treated his slaves badly. He often beat them without provocation.

His wife was about to give birth to their first child. One of his slaves, Hosea, was a gifted carpenter, so Jacob asked him to create a chest of drawers for his baby's belongings. Hosea worked long and hard on the chest and was pleased with his labor, but Cooley was not happy with the results.

It is unclear why Cooley was so unhappy. One look at this Empire-style mahogany chest of drawers clearly reveals fine craftsmanship. Was this not what Cooley envisioned? Even if there had been a miscommunication, there is no excuse for Cooley's reaction. He berated Hosea and beat him so badly that he died a few days later as a result of his injuries.

The other slaves and Hosea's family were angry over Hosea's senseless death. They were also angry that Cooley had placed the chest in the nursery. If he was so displeased with the chest, why did he have it moved into the baby's room? They thought he didn't have any problem with the chest, he was just an angry man who got pleasure out of abusing his slaves. Perhaps he had agreed to compensate the slave for his efforts but faked dissatisfaction to avoid holding up his end of the bargain.

The other slaves wanted retribution. They asked a slave who was gifted in conjuring to place a curse on the chest as payback for what happened to Hosea. A conjurer is someone who conjures spirits or practices [black] magic. Owl's blood was sprinkled inside the drawers, and a chant accompanied the ritual to complete the curse. All *future* generations of this family would suffer the curse, the conjurer assumed them.

It began with Jacob's son. His first child was also the son he desperately wanted. Sadly, the baby died during his infancy. Another son was born, only to be stabbed to death by a servant. Jacob's youngest daughter, Melinda, inherited the chest. Soon after, her husband abandoned her and their children. He ran away to New Orleans. Heartbroken and despondent, Melinda died a short time later. The family received word that her husband had died in a freak accident soon after arriving in New Orleans.

One of their orphaned children inherited the chest. It sat empty for many years, so nothing bad happened. Apparently, the curse was only active once something was placed in the chest of drawers. Melinda's daughter, Arabella, stored her wedding dress in the chest for safe storage—or so they thought. Arabella's husband died soon afterward. Arabella was pregnant with their first child. As the birth date got close, Arabella began getting ready for the baby. She got the nursery ready and placed some baby clothes in the chest. The baby lived only a few weeks before mysteriously dying.

The stories go on and on. One family tragedy after another. A hunting accident. Stabbed to death. A terminal childhood illness. A fatal fall. Finally, a family member, Virginia Hudson, came to believe the chest was cursed and that the curse must be broken once and for all. She hired her own conjurer, asking her to undo the curse. The old African-American woman said that would only be possible if three conditions were met:

1. The conjurer would have to receive an owl without asking for one.
2. The young leaves of a willow tree had to be collected and boiled all day in a large pot.
3. The boiled concoction had to be placed in a jug facing East underneath a flowering bush. Throughout this process, the owl must remain within sight of the conjurer.

Remarkably, these tasks were all achieved, and the potion was sprinkled inside each drawer. She also placed an envelope in the top drawer of the chest. No one in the Cooley family died prematurely or due to unusual circumstances. The old conjurer died later that year of natural causes.

So did this ritual reverse the spell? Since no one ever put anything inside the chest ever again, it is not known for certain if the curse was removed or is just dormant. Even though all of this had been done so as to remove the family curse, the chest was stored in an attic for many years so that no one would use it. Eventually, it was donated to a museum in 1976.

There is allegedly an envelope in the top drawer of the conjure chest containing the feathers of that owl used to reverse the curse. The museum has left it where the conjurer put it with the idea that it is better safe than sorry.

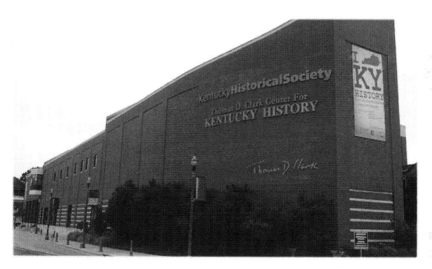

The museum has many interesting exhibits, including "Kentucky during the Victorian Age" and the "Hall of Governors." The facility also boasts a premier research library.

Crying Boy

Location: United Kingdom

Origin: 1950s

Visitor Information: None

About The Haunted Object: Comprehensive research and evidence are often hard to come by when exploring paranormal activity. Much of your information is pieced together through second-hand witness statements and stories. Even when you are lucky enough to be a part of a paranormal investigation, you only have one piece of the puzzle as you only have that one particular experience that occurs at one specific time and date. These difficulties are compounded when researching haunted objects.

There is no way to conduct your own experiment or investigation. You must rely on whatever information you can collect and then try to verify it as best you can. In this case, there are many conflicting accounts and not much more than hearsay to go on. But here is what I discovered and you can decide for yourself what to believe.

It begins with a painting of a crying boy. I'm not sure what would appeal to an artist about rendering such a painting, but I suppose an artist might find it artistically fulfilling to create such a thing. However, I am stymied as to why anyone would want to own such a sad, strange painting.

The artist, Bruno Amadio, painted *The Crying Boy* in the 1950s. The painting was then mass produced and sold commercially at many locations throughout the United Kingdom. But then something strange happened.

A mass of house fires broke out in Yorkshire and Rotherham, and the only thing that wasn't destroyed in these homes was *The Crying Boy* painting. It was found in perfect condition still hanging on what was left of the wall. This did not go unnoticed by firefighters. One firefighter, Alan Wilkinson, logged more than fifty of these house fires. Firefighters can be superstitious, so no firefighter in this area would permit this painting to be hung in their homes. In fact, when Wilkinson retired, some of his men gave him this painting as a joke. He refused to accept it. Instead, he displayed it at his old firehouse, but his supervisor made him take it down. He was also a superstitious man and wasn't about to tempt fate.

As word grew about the connection between the painting and all the house fires, folks got spooked. The British newspaper, *The Sun*, offered a solution. They organized a big bonfire and invited the public to bring their paintings. They were going to burn all the *Crying Boy* paintings and hopefully stop the fires. Reportedly, more than 2,500 prints were collected that night.

According to some sources, the boy in the painting was a street orphan from Madrid named Don Bonillo. The villagers called him Diablo, which means "Devil." They said he was a bad seed, but Amadio felt sorry for the child. He adopted him against the advice of a local priest. Some say Diablo haunts the painting, angry at how cruelly the world has treated him. It is rumored that Amadio abused the child. If so, maybe the priest was trying to protect the child rather than Amadio by discouraging the adoption.

Not long after the adoption was finalized, Amadio's studio burned to the ground. At least one account claims Amadio made the boy leave after this incident.

The house fires stopped as abruptly as they started, but many think the paintings were still cursed. There were many tragic, sometimes bizarre, deaths associated with the paintings. Some shared their stories with *The Sun*. Here is an excerpt from one such letter, "*Since I bought it, my three sons and my husband have all died. I've often wondered if it had a curse.*" -Rose Farrington

Typically, it is one object that is haunted by one person who has a connection with the object. This is hundreds or thousands of paintings. Is this possible or is this just a really big coincidence?

In another odd aspect of this story, the artist had several pseudonyms, which makes research challenging. Bruno Amadio also went by the names Franchot Seville, Giovanni Bragolin, Angelo Giovanni Bragolin, and J. Bragolin. There may have been more pseudonyms. So why would he use all these names? One popular theory is that his name became synonymous with the cursed painting, so no one wanted to buy his art. They were fearful of another curse, so Amadio kept creating aliases to sell his work.

As if this story wasn't strange enough, it seems that Amadio painted more than one boy. He painted several different boys, all reportedly street orphans like Diablo. But is that true? Amadio once did a television interview in which he claimed all his painting were of dead children. He tried to capture their sad spirits on canvas and may have inadvertently captured something far more sinister.

He didn't just paint boys. He also painted little girls, but not nearly as often as he painted little boys. Oddly, there are no curses associated with the girl paintings. One of his little girl painting is allegedly Diablo's sister.

Here is a letter I uncovered while researching this story:

"...my great grandfather lived in Davenport in the early 1980s. His house was old but always clean and safe because he frequently had children visiting. The only thing that scared me in my grandfather's house was this creepy close up of a boy crying. I was a young boy at the time and didn't like the fact that it felt like the boy was watching me. Anyway, in the summer of 1983 he left town for a business trip and returned to find his house had burnt to the ground. Searching through remains of his home he found that only two things had survived the fire: a photo album of me and that painting. He told me this story several times before he died but I never believe him, thinking he was just trying to spook me. I am 23 now and when I read this story, more than just a chill ran down my spine. I once asked my grandfather what happened to the painting and he said he sold it for a dollar at a garage sale. I remember the painting but not the fire..." Steve

According to art experts, *The Crying Boy* prints are not valuable, but *The Crying Girl* prints can fetch anywhere from $5,000 - $10,000, presumably because there are fewer of these paintings. Over the years, psychics have been asked to do their thing. Most of these psychics claim the painting is haunted by the spirit of the boy it depicts.

Note: Some believe the paintings were treated with a fire retardant varnish and that is why they survived the fires when everything else perished.

Dibbuk Box

Location: Unknown

Origin: Europe

Visitor Information: None

About The Haunted Object: This story begins around 1930. A World War I Holocaust survivor named Haleva immigrated to America. She brought her few belongings with her, including an antique box. According to some sources, the box was a family heirloom that survived the war. According to other sources, Haleva acquired the box before she left Europe. I believe the former is true as it doesn't make sense that she would buy such a large item while moving to another continent. It makes more sense that it was a family heirloom she was safeguarding—and for a good reason.

This was not any old box. It is a dibbuk box, also known as a dybbuk box. To be exact, it is a small wine cabinet haunted by a dibbuk. The box was never opened so as not to free the dibbuk.

FYI: About a dibbuk…This is a Hebrew word meaning "cling." According to Jewish folklore, a dibbuk is an evil spirit that clings or attaches itself to an object or person.

TERRANCE ZEPKE
SPOOKIEST OBJECTS

When Haleva died at age 103 in 2003, her belongings were auctioned off during an estate sale. The antique dealer handling the sale, Kevin Mannis, asked the family if they wanted to keep any heirlooms or personal belongings, such as the wine cabinet. They assured him they did not. The family knew the history of the box and just wanted rid of it. However, the devout Jews felt an obligation to reveal its dark backstory. They told Mannis about the dibbuk and that they just wanted rid of it. They said the box must be a part of the sale or the auction was off.

Mannis ended up keeping the box. Records don't indicate whether he was unable to sell it or if he ethically had a problem selling a dibbuk box or if he simply liked it and wanted it for himself. Whatever the case, he took the cabinet back to his store.

Shortly after that, a hysterical employee phoned him. She said she had arrived at work and discovered something strange was going on. She said the doors were locked, so she didn't see how anyone could have gotten in, but she could hear noises inside Mannis' office. His office was locked, and she didn't have a key, not that she would have tried to enter after hearing the commotion on the other side of the door. She said all the light bulbs had been smashed and there was a strange odor in the building.

Mannis raced over to his store to find out what was going on. He found the broken light bulbs and smelled the strange odor, which has been described as smelling like cat urine. He unlocked his office and found no one and nothing out of place. An inventory check revealed nothing had been taken. There was no logical explanation as to what had happened. There were no signs of an intruder or a break in, but what about all the broken light bulbs and bizarre smell? Also, the employee was adamant she heard someone in her boss's office. In fact, she was so unnerved by the incident that she quit. She said there was no way she could work alone in the building anymore after what had happened.

Mannis was confounded by the incident but dismissed it in due course since nothing had been taken and no harm had occurred. Soon after that, he inspected the old wine cabinet. When he opened it to examine its interior and its contents, here is what he found:

*Two 1920s pennies

*a lock of blond hair wrapped around a cord

*a lock of black hair wrapped around a cord

*a wine goblet

*a dried rose bud

*a candle holder

*a small statue engraved with the word "Shalom" on it

These sound like items used to perform a ceremony or ritual, presumably to trap the dibbuk in the box.

Mannis didn't find anything that seemed overly bizarre, but he had opened the box. He had released the evil entity. That's when the nightmares and eerie encounters began. He began having bad dreams about demons. At the time, he didn't connect the nightmares with the box. He just thought he was having bad dreams as people do from time to time. He gave the box to his mother as a birthday gift. That night she suffered a stroke. She knew right away there was a connection. She told her son she didn't want the box. She demanded he come and get it immediately.

Mannis honored his mother's wishes, but by this time, he decided he didn't want the box back either. He gave it to his sister, who returned it less than a week later. Next, it went to Kevin's brother, who soon decided he didn't want it either. Mannis once again had possession of the dibbuk box. He sold it to a couple, but found it in front of his store one morning with a note saying *This has a bad darkness.*

Mannis was confounded as to what to do. He was afraid to keep the box and afraid to get rid of it. He wanted to destroy it but wasn't sure what might happen to him if he did. So he did the only thing he could think of, he listed it for sale on eBay, the online auction site. He included an explanation about the box and why he was getting rid of it. Remarkably, it sold and has sold several times since the initial sale. All owners reported supernatural activity and a strange odor.

Finally, the cabinet was sold to Jason Haxton, who is the director of the Museum of Osteopathic Medicine. Shortly after taking possession of the cursed object, he began to have health problems. His hair began falling out for no medical reason, at least none the doctors could diagnosis. He suffered other health issues and doctors were unable to determine the underlying cause. He had been perfectly healthy until he had taken possession of the dibbuk box.

Also, he kept finding smashed light bulbs and an odd odor. Like previous owners, he also saw shadowy figures and heard unexplainable noises. The last straw was when he awoke one night to find a strange figure leaving his bedroom. He watched in disbelief as it disappeared into the wall! The cabinet doors would not stay shut no matter what. Even when he firmly closed them and they clicked shut, he later found them wide open.

Sensing a connection between the box and all these incidents, Haxton reached out to Kevin Mannis for help. He explained all that had transpired and begged Mannis to work with him to uncover the history of the box. He felt that was the key to stopping this evil entity. Mannis reluctantly agreed. The family put the men in touch with an elderly aunt of Haleva's named Sophia. What she told them was shocking.

Sophia revealed that she and Havela had been playing with a spirit board one night. They realized they had inadvertently summoned an evil spirit—a dibbuk. They were unable to send it back, but they were able to trap it inside the old cabinet. When Havela migrated to the U.S., she brought the cabinet to ensure the dibbuk stayed locked inside. And she managed to safeguard everyone until her death.

Jason Haxton hired a psychic to see what kind of energy she felt coming from the box. Shortly after the psychic sat down and began her ritual, she touched the box. Instantly, she felt a stabbing pain all over, especially in her head and chest. She sensed the pain was connected to the original owner of the box. She also sensed fear and death associated with the box.

So it seems the only question left is "How to put the genie back in the bottle?" or in this case "How to put the dibbuk back in the box?

Haxton consulted several Rabbis, explaining the situation. They told him what he needed to do to get the dibbuk back in the box and keep it there. This included making an ark of acacia wood and gold. It should be a replica of the Ark of the Covenant, which contained the Ten Commandments. This was a holy box, which was the only thing that could contain a dibbuk, according to the Rabbis.

Jason Haxton did as he was instructed and has hidden the dibbuk box in an undisclosed location. He has vowed never to tell anyone where it is and to safeguard the box as long as he lives. The question remains, "What will happen when Jason Haxton is no longer able to safeguard the box?

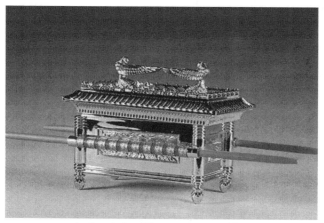

Ark of the Covenant replica

GODDESS OF DEATH

Goddess of Death

Location: National Museum of Scotland

Origin: Circa 3500 B.C.E.

Visitor Information: The museum is free and OPEN TO THE PUBLIC every day but Christmas Day. There are shops and restaurants inside the museum, in addition to exhibits. Chambers Street, Edinburgh Scotland EH1 1JF http://www.nms.ac.uk/national-museum-of-scotland/plan-your-visit/

About The Haunted Object: I'm not certain when the hauntings began because this statue dates back to 3500 B.C. Known originally as the Woman from Lemb, this statue is now commonly referred to as the Goddess of Death. The statue was discovered in Lemb, Cypress in 1878. That's about all we know for certain.

It is believed that the limestone statue is a fertility idol, although it is hard to tell by its appearance. Everyone who has come into possession of this statue has suffered untimely deaths.

The first we know of is Lord Elphont. Without six years of owning the statue, all seven members of his family were deceased.

The next owner was Ivor Manucci. His family suffered the same fate. All were dead less than four years after Manucci brought the statue into their home.

Lord Thompson-Noel was the next owner. Again, he and his entire family died less than four years from the day they took possession of the statue.

After that, Sir Alan Biverbrook acquired the Lemb Statue. His wife and two daughters died soon after that. The destructive, deathly cycle was finally broken when Biverbrook donated the statue to the Royal Scottish Museum (now the National Museum of Scotland) rather than sell it to another buyer.

It was placed in a locked, glass case. Everyone hoped this would end the curse. Sadly, the curator who handled the statue died shortly after that. No one has touched the statue since that time. It has remained in a locked case. And there has been no further activity by the Goddess of Death.

National Museum of Scotland

FYI: The museum was the most visited attraction in Scotland last year. It houses artifacts from around the world, including archaeology, natural history, science, geology, technology, art, and world cultures. There are more than 8,000 intriguing objects, such as the stuffed body of Dolly the sheep, which was the first successful clone of a mammal. You'll also find an Elton John exhibit, Ancient Egypt exhibit, and a Scottish invention called The Maiden, which is a guillotine of sorts.

Hope Diamond

Location: Washington, DC

Origin: It has been on display in a museum since 1958, but reportedly dates back to the 1600s.

Visitor Information: The diamond can be seen in the Smithsonian Gem Collection in the Natural History Museum of the Smithsonian. It is OPEN TO THE PUBLIC every day 10 a.m. – 5:30 p.m. except Christmas Day, with no admission fee charged. The Smithsonian Visitor Center is located at 1000 Jefferson Dr., SW, Washington, D.C. Most of the Smithsonian museums can be found on 3rd to 14th Streets between Constitution Avenue and Independence Avenue. The Natural History Museum is at 10th Street. www.si.edu and www.naturalhistory.si.edu.

About The Haunted Object: This is probably the most famous haunted object in the world. Most of us have heard stories about the Hope Diamond, but do we know the real story?

This story goes back to 1642. A French jeweler, Jean Baptiste Tavernier, found a diamond while traveling in India. But this wasn't just any old diamond. It was an 112-carat blue diamond. It came from Kollur Mine in Golconda, India.

Or did it? According to legend, the diamond was stolen from an Indian idol, which is when the curse began. Whatever its origins and whether you believe in cursed objects or not, there is no disputing this was a perfect gem. It was enormous, perfect quality, and the rarest color. As far as diamonds go, this one was off the charts for the four "C's": color, cut, carat, and clarity.

When he returned to France, Tavernier sold the spectacular diamond to King Louis XIV. The king was so pleased that he made Tavernier a noble.

The king ultimately had the diamond cut to reflect its true brilliance. It was so big and dense that it didn't dazzle and sparkle to the king's satisfaction. The new size was sixty-seven carats. The precious jewel became known as the Blue Diamond of the Crown. The king had it set in gold and wore it around his neck on a long ribbon.

The crown jewel was stolen from the Garde-Meuble during the French Revolution. It showed up in London in 1813 and ever since that time it has been known as the Cursed Diamond.

The gem changed hands several times, but the same grim ending is true for every owner, from King George IV to Henry Hope. The king had so many debts upon his death that the Crown was forced to sell the gem. Henry Philip Hope went bankrupt after obtaining the diamond.

Jeweler Pierre Cartier showed Evalyn Walsh McLean the diamond in 1910 while visiting Paris, but she didn't care for it! Cartier had the diamond reset in a fancier setting and presented it to McLean once again. He told her to keep it for the weekend. The jeweler was convinced that the diamond would grow on McLean in time. He was right. At the end of the weekend, the socialite bought the stunning diamond for $180,000.

Evalyn McLean was another owner who suffered great loss after acquiring the diamond. Her daughter committed suicide, her nine-year-old son died in an auto accident, her husband was institutionalized, and Evalyn had to undergo goiter surgery shortly after she acquired the diamond. Is it a coincidence the diamond was positioned precisely on her throat where surgery was required? The family went bankrupt and was forced to sell their newspaper, *The Washington Post*, and most of their properties.

The family sold all of Evalyn's jewelry to settle the estate, including the diamond necklace. It was sold to a renowned jeweler, Harry Winston, in 1949. Shockingly, Winston donated the necklace to the Smithsonian Institution. Some say Winston had long wanted to create a national jewelry collection. Others claim he donated the necklace to end the curse. Regardless, it was a coup for the museum and the end of a long curse. It arrived at the Smithsonian in a plain, brown envelope via registered mail. The famous jewels have been on display at our nation's largest museum since 1958.

FYI: When you visit the Smithsonian, you're entering the world's largest museum, education, and research complex, with approximately 154 million artifacts and specimens in its trust for the American people. The Smithsonian offers eleven museums and galleries on the National Mall and six other museums and the National Zoo in the greater National Capital Area.

Gems & Minerals Gallery of Smithsonian

Fun Facts

The Hope Diamond is the largest deep blue diamond in the world.

It is surrounded by sixteen white pear-shaped and cushion-cut diamonds hanging from a chain that contains forty-five diamonds.

The diamond is one of the most popular exhibits in the Smithsonian. More than six million people visit the Hope Diamond exhibit each year.

Jeweler Harry Winston donated the Hope Diamond to the Smithsonian in 1958. It arrived in a plain, brown envelope by registered mail. It was insured for $1 million. Today, it has a value of $200 - $250 million.

The Hope diamond has left the Smithsonian four times since it was donated. In 1962, it was exhibited for a month at The Louvre in Paris, France. In 1965, the Hope diamond traveled to South Africa where it was exhibited at the Rand Easter Show in Johannesburg. In 1984, the diamond was lent to Harry Winston Inc., in New York, as part of the firm's 50th anniversary celebration. In 1996, the Hope diamond was again sent to Harry Winston Inc. for cleaning and restoration work.

FYI: Another famously haunted gem is the Delhi Purple Sapphire, which is on display in London's Natural History Museum. It is unknown why it is called a purple sapphire since it is an amethyst, but this is just one of many bizarre facets to the story. The jewel was stolen from a temple in India. It had adorned the Hindu Goddess of Weather and War before it was stolen by Colonel W. Ferris, who fell on hard times soon after acquiring the stone. Since that time, all its owners have suffered horrible fates that include losing their vast fortunes and good health. The last owner, Edward Heron-Allen, bestowed the precious gem to the museum with the stipulation that the box would not be opened until three years after his death and that his daughter would never be permitted to touch the cursed jewel or take possession of it. He claimed the Delhi Purple Sapphire was "trebly accursed and is stained with the blood, and the dishonor of everyone who has ever owned it." He was so convinced of the object was cursed that he sealed it inside seven boxes with protective charms and left a warning note, "*Whoever shall then open it, shall first read out this warning, and then do as he pleases with the jewel. My advice to him or her is to cast it into the sea.*"

Myrtles Mirror

Location: St. Francisville, Louisiana

Origin: Unknown

Visitor Information: It is OPEN TO THE PUBLIC. The old plantation is listed on the National Register of Historic Places and Myrtles Plantation is now a bed and breakfast inn. History and mystery tours are offered. There are guest rooms in the plantation house and elsewhere on the grounds. There is also a restaurant that is open every day except Tuesdays.

7747 US Hwy 61, St. Francisville, LA 70775 (22 miles north of Baton Rouge Airport)

www.myrtlesplantation.com

About The Haunted Object: This story begins with a man named David Bradford, who married Elizabeth Porter in 1785. When the couple began having children, they needed a larger residence, one that could double as a home and law office for David Bradford.

Things went well for the Bradford family until David got involved in the Whiskey Rebellion. Farmers used excess grain and corn to make whiskey to subsidize their income. When the government began taxing it in 1791, farmers throughout Pennsylvania protested the new tax. One of the men who joined the protest was General David "Whiskey Dave" Bradford.

When President George Washington sent militia to Pennsylvania to squash the rebellion, Bradford decided it was in his best interest to leave. He fled, ending up in Louisiana, after making a brief stop in Pittsburgh to settle his family. He had to distance himself from his family since he was a wanted man who was hiding from the law.

During this time, Bradford bought 600 acres of land in Louisiana and built an eight-room house in 1796 that he called "Laurel Grove." In 1799, he received a pardon for his participation in the Whiskey Rebellion from newly elected President John Adams. He immediately retrieved his wife and five kids from Pittsburgh and brought them to Laurel Grove.

Sadly, all of his children, except his daughter Sarah, died of yellow fever. Bradford gave up his law practice and now mentored law students, including a young man named Clark Woodrooff. Woodrooff fell in love with Sarah Bradford, and they were married on November 19, 1817.

When David Bradford died, the house was left to his wife, Elizabeth, but it was Clark and Sarah Woodrooff who took care of the property. It was a big responsibility considering the size of the plantation. The 650-acre plantation produced lucrative cotton and indigo crops.

Sarah and Clark had three children, who were cared for by a slave girl named Chloe. And this is where the story gets interesting. Clark

Woodrooff bought the plantation from his mother-in-law, although she continued to live there until her death in 1830. As his law practice grew, Clark found it difficult to meet the incessant demands of running a big plantation. He preferred practicing law to farming, so he hired an overseer and devoted his full attention to pursuing his legal career. His hard work paid off when he was appointed as a judge.

Clark Woodrooff changed his name to Woodruff and sold Laurel Grove to Ruffin Stirling on January 1, 1834. Ruffin Stirling and his wife, Mary, made major renovations to the property and changed the name to "The Myrtles." They traveled to Europe to find just the right furnishings for their home, which had doubled in size due to their extensive remodeling. Just four years after the renovations were completed, Ruffin died of consumption, more commonly known today as tuberculosis.

Mary gave the property to her daughter, Sarah, and husband, William Winter. It was devastating when the home was lost to bankruptcy just a few years later. However, in an odd turn of events, Sarah found the resources to buy back the plantation just two years later. William and Sarah and the widower Mary returned to their beloved home.

Life was good until January 1871 when a man on horseback approached the house. He shouted, *"William Winter! Are you home, William Winter?"* William, who was in one of the parlors at the time, heard the summons and went outside to see what was going on. As soon as he stepped onto the porch, the man on horseback shot him without ever dismounting. The killer sped away on his horse immediately after the fatal shooting. The murder was never solved, and Sarah never got over her husband's death. Despite the tragic event, Sarah and her mother continued to live at The Myrtles until Sarah's death in 1878. Her mother, Mary Stirling, died two years later.

The home then came under the ownership of Stephen Stirling, who was unable to keep the family home. Accounts vary as to whether Stephen went bankrupt or lost the property during a card game.

Whatever the case, the house had several owners over the next several decades until the 1950s when it was bought by Marjorie Munson.

This was when the paranormal activity that previous owners had kept secret became public. There have been hundreds of reports of unexplainable footsteps on the stairs, piano music, mysterious smells (including the smell of gunfire), objects that have been moved, and ghost sightings. A young woman in a long white dress or nightgown has been seen. She reportedly died despite being treated by a voodoo practitioner, but her spirit still lingers at the old plantation. Some claim to have seen the ghost of William Winter. A Native American woman has been seen. Since research shows the house was built on top of a Native American burial ground, this makes sense.

During the Civil War, the house was ransacked by Union soldiers, and legend claims that the three men were killed in the house. There have supposedly been ten murders on the property, but only one, the shooting of William Winter, can be substantiated with indisputable historical evidence. So were there other murders or is this part of the story pure fiction? If the story about the murders of Sara Woodruff, her two children, and Chloe are true, then it may add up to ten murders. We may never know anything more given that the house is well over 200 years old, has had dozens of owners, and many records have been lost over time. What we do know is that most famous ghost at Myrtles is Chloe.

Chloe was a slave who had an affair with Clark Woodruff. The affair allegedly began while Sarah Woodruff was bedridden during her third pregnancy. After the child was born, Clark ended the affair. Chloe feared that she would be sent to work in the fields now that the affair was over. She began spying on the family, hoping to learn some useful information. Sounds like she was prepared to blackmail Woodruff if it came to it.

But Clark caught Chloe spying and was furious. According to legend, he had one of her ears cut off to show his slaves what happens to eavesdroppers. Chloe was forced to wear a green turban for the rest of her life to hide the deformity. This is when Chloe came up with a diabolical plan. Chloe poisoned the family by adding finely grounded oleander flowers into a birthday cake batter. Oleander is highly toxic. Chloe figured that everyone in the family would eat a slice of the little girl's birthday cake. We will never know if she meant to kill them or just make the family very ill. Regardless of her intent, Sarah and two of her children died within hours of eating the cake. Ironically, the person she despised the most, Clark Woodruff, didn't eat any cake, so he never had so much as a stomach ache.

Another slave discovered what Chloe had done and told some of the other slaves. They were fearful that the poisoning would be discovered and the wrong person blamed. During the night, the group of slaves came for Chloe. They hanged her. Later, they disposed of the body in the nearby river. Many believe that her angry spirit still haunts Myrtles, seeking retribution. Some say this is all folklore that never happened. According to some, Sarah and the children died of yellow fever, not poisoning.

If that were true, then why does owner Marjorie Munson swear she has seen a ghostly figure wearing a green bonnet on many occasions? Unaware of Chloe or her fate, Munson began researching the property. That's when she learned the story about Chloe and her green turban.

According to the Myrtles Planation website, photographs were taken in 1992 of the property for insurance purposes. One of the photographs showed something most unusual and unexplainable. The image revealed what appeared to be a slave girl standing between two buildings. National Geographic authenticated the photograph, declaring they believed it to be authentic and agreeing that it seemed to be a slave girl standing in the breezeway between two buildings.

But even if you don't believe all the accounts of paranormal activity, there is one thing that is impossible to dispute. The plantation has a haunted object—a mirror. Many visitors have photographed the famous mirror during their stay at Myrtles Plantation. Many of their photographs have revealed some strange things. Child-sized handprints often appear in the images where the photographers swear they saw nothing in the mirror when they took the photos. Also, ghostly figures have been seen in the mirror.

It is believed that the handprints and figures belong to Sarah, Chloe, and the two Woodruff children who died as a result of Chloe's poisoning (or possibly from yellow fever). However they died, their deaths were tragic.

According to folklore, when there was a death, all mirrors were supposed to be covered to prevent spirits from being trapped. Somehow this mirror was never covered when Sarah and her children died. And it wasn't covered when Chloe was hanged. Many speculate that because this custom wasn't observed, their spirits were trapped and now they haunt or curse that mirror and Myrtles Plantation.

Regardless of whether you believe the stories and paranormal activity at Myrtles or you do not, it is hard to contradict what has been witnessed and documented involving this mirror. There is no doubt that it is one of the most haunted objects in the world. Even though the mirror has been moved from the dining room to the hallway and despite the glass being cleaned—and even replaced—this mirror continues to reveal small handprints and ghostly figures seemingly stuck inside the glass. Who they are and why they are there may be ambiguous, but the hundreds of sightings cannot be contested.

FYI: Strange things happened while a movie was shot at the Myrtles. During the filming of the movie, *The Long Hot Summer* (starring Don Johnson, Ava Gardner, Cybill Shepherd, and Jason Robards), the crew encountered paranormal activity. At the end of the day, they moved furniture for a scene that was to be shot the next morning. When they arrived to shoot the scene, they found that all the furniture had been moved back to its original location. The place had been secured for the shoot, so this baffled all involved. They restaged the room, but before they could shoot the scene, they discovered the furniture had been moved again. This happened several times before they were finally able to guard the room and shoot the scene. A guard assigned to keep folks away during filming watched a young woman in an old-fashioned white dress walk through the gate and up to the house. She did not acknowledge him. He chased after her to tell her she would have to leave. Before he could catch up to her, he watched her "walk" right through the front door! He was so shaken by this event that he quit his job and never went near the house again. Most of the cast and crew admitted they were glad when taping was over, and they could leave Myrtles Plantation.

In 2002, *Unsolved Mysteries* filmed a segment about the alleged hauntings at the plantation. According to host Robert Stack, the production crew experienced numerous technical difficulties during the production of the segment. The Myrtles was also featured on a 2005 episode of *Ghost Hunters*.

The William Winter Room is located on the second floor of the mansion. This is the room where Cleo, a local voodoo priestess, was brought in hopes of saving a child who was severely ill with Scarlet Fever. But the voodoo priestess was not able to prevent the child's death. The room is one of the most haunted areas of the old plantation.

A page on the inn's website is devoted to paranormal activity reported by guests and visitors, http://www.myrtlesplantation.com/haunts.php.

Mystery tours are offered: http://www.myrtlesplantation.com/tours.php.

Robert the Doll

Location: Fort East Martello Museum (Key West, Florida)

Origin: 1904

Visitor Information: The museum is OPEN TO THE PUBLIC. Fort East Martello Museum is at 3501 S. Roosevelt Blvd. Key West, FL 33040.

www.robertthedoll.org/visit

About The Haunted Object: Robert Eugene "Gene" Otto was given a doll by a family servant. According to legend, the Bahamian servant practiced black magic (voodoo), and she did not like the Otto family. Some believe she cursed the doll before giving it to the little boy. They think she conjured an evil entity that attached itself to the doll. After reading this story, you may come to agree with this assessment.

Gene named the doll Robert and the boy and his doll became inseparable. Gene carried Robert the doll everywhere; the way kids do with beloved stuffed animals or dolls. His parents often heard Gene talking with someone in his bedroom. They heard two distinctly different voices. Thinking that Gene had a friend in his room, they went to check on the boys. Each time they found only Gene and Robert. In time, they came to believe that the other voice they heard that they did not recognize was Robert's. Strange as it sounds, they thought the doll was conversing with their son.

In what has now become a famous Key West saying and postcard greeting, the parents often heard their son saying "*Robert did it!*" This was the reaction they got from their son when they reprimanded him for bad behavior. When they found a vase smashed, furniture knocked over, or items scattered across a room, they blamed their son. There was no other logical explanation unless you believe "*Robert did it!*"

Neighbors wouldn't doubt Robert did it. They reported seeing the doll move from window to window when the family was out. Neighbors aren't the only witnesses. Over the years, many others claim to have seen the doll move. A plumber once noticed the doll as he entered the house. While he was working, he heard giggling behind him. Assuming it was a child, he turned around to give a greeting. Imagine his surprise to discover the only thing in the room besides him was the doll that he had seen in the other room. It had seemingly transported itself across the house! Visitors often reported a strange feeling when near the doll. They couldn't explain themselves except to say they felt the doll was watching them, perhaps trying to communicate with them or get their attention.

Some even swore the doll's stoic facial expression changed.

Gene Otto lived in the house with Robert the doll until his death in 1974. Myrtle Reuter bought the house and discovered the doll in the attic. Thinking it was cute, she put it in one of the bedrooms. But she kept discovering the doll in different places than where she had left it. This happened many times. She never saw the doll move, but she made a note of where she left it only to discover it on another floor of the house! She also heard footsteps overhead at times when no one else was in the house. She also heard giggling on occasion.

Myrtle was understandably freaked out by the unexplainable noises and doll movement. Ultimately, she donated Robert the Doll to the East Martello Museum. Coincidentally, Gene Otto had designed the museum gallery where Robert the Doll now resides.

Since the doll took up residence in the museum, the staff have felt a definitive shift in energy. For lack of a better way to explain it, the vibe changed inside the museum. Visitors have also reported strange encounters with the doll. Cameras often malfunction and museum lights now flicker inexplicably. Many visitors have experienced a series of "unfortunately incidents" in their lives after photographing the doll without permission. Letters arrive throughout the year from visitors begging Robert for forgiveness and apologizing for any disrespectful behavior on their part.

So if you visit Robert the Doll, it might be best to ask permission before photographing him. To be on the safe side, it might be best not to take any photos or do anything else that may be construed as disrespectful.

About Robert the Doll

According to the Key West Historical Society, Robert is a handmade doll, crafted by the Steiff Company of Germany. He is forty inches tall and stuffed with wood wool (excelsior). He is dressed in a sailor suit. He is displayed in a locked glass case. He served as inspiration for the creepy Chucky doll in the Chucky horror movie series. Some sources claim the doll is stuffed with straw and was made by a Haitian or Bahamian servant that practiced voodoo.

FYI: There are several companies that offer ghost tours of Key West, which is considered to be one of the most haunted cities in America. The Hemingway House & Museum, Hard Rock Café, Key West Cemetery, Captain Tony's Saloon, and Fort Zachary Taylor are among the most haunted places in Key West. Type "list of ghost walks in Key West" into any search engine to get a comprehensive list of options.

Royal Chairs of Belcourt

Location: Newport, Rhode Island

Origin: The house was built in 1894; the chairs once belonged to French royalty, but the date of origin is unknown.

Visitor Information: The house was sold by Mrs. Tinney in 2012. It is privately owned and not open to the public. However, special seasonal tours are given, such as their candlelight ghost tours during the fall.

657 Bellevue Avenue. Newport, Rhode Island 02840

www.belcourt.com.

About The Haunted Object: Newport is one of the oldest towns in America, dating back to 1690. It is home to some of the wealthiest families in America, which means there are many mansions here. One such mansion is Belcourt Castle. After three years of construction, the sixty-room, three-story, 50,000-square foot castle was completed.

This is a spectacular place to have such humble beginnings. The "Belcourt" began as a hunting lodge. The original plan called for one bedroom and one bathroom. There was no kitchen, but there was a huge stable and sleeping quarters for all the servants. Reportedly, he had thirty horses and thirty servants in the early days at Belcourt. His racing horses were given only the best. They each had comfortable stalls and slept on fine linens imported from Ireland.

Somehow this simple plan ballooned into a 50,000 square-foot edifice that included sixty rooms. It was designed by renowned architect Richard M. Hunt in a Louis XIII French Renaissance style and required

300 European craftsmen to build it. A kitchen was eventually built but not in the house as Oliver was terribly afraid that a fire might break out in the kitchen and destroy the home. He built the kitchen in another building and food was delivered by carriage to the main house. There are tunnels that extended from the house to the kitchen so that servants could easily go back and forth. It cost three million dollars and three and a half years to complete (1891 – 1894). The price tag is equivalent to over seventy million today. No wonder ghosts choose to linger here!

This may seem extravagant for a hunting retreat, but not to its owner. Oliver Belmont was born on November 12, 1858. His father was a banker and one of the richest men in the world. At 24, Oliver married Sara Swan Whiting, but the pair divorced that same year. Sara gave birth to a baby girl soon after the divorce became final. Oliver never saw his daughter, who died in her 20s.

Oliver Hazard Perry Belmont inherited sixty million dollars in 1890, so money was no object. In addition to being very wealthy, the bachelor had many other appealing qualities. He was a graduate of Annapolis Naval Academy, had served one term as a Congressman, belonged to all the right social clubs, and had lots of interesting hobbies.

Oliver eventually remarried. Of all the women he could have had, Oliver ended up marrying his best friend's ex-wife, Anna Vanderbilt, less than one year after the divorce. She was responsible for many renovations in the house. Reportedly, she had the Grand Staircase moved four times before the workmen refused to do it anymore. What's even more amazing is that the Belmonts only stayed in this house eight weeks out of each year.

When Oliver died in 1908, Anna threw herself into politics, especially women's' rights. And she enjoyed traveling and living the good life. At one point, she owned nine estates!

She chose her favorite for retirement, a chateau in France. She lived there until her death in 1933 at the age of 80. She would have lived longer had she not suffered certain injuries during a carriage accident. She was buried next to Oliver in the Belmont family mausoleum in New York.

Oliver's nineteen-year-old nephew, August Belmont IV inherited Belcourt. But it ended up in the possession of Oliver's last surviving brother, who sold it in 1940. Belcourt was no longer in the Belmont family for the first time in its history. And it changed ownership several more times until 1956 when it was bought by Harold B. Tinney. The Tinney family drove by the vacant mansion and knew immediately that they wanted it. They bought it at the bargain price of $25,000 since the chateau had deteriorated greatly by that time.

The following year it became Belcourt Castle and a public museum. The Tinney family appreciated the beauty of the mansion. They made many renovations to the rundown property and delighted in furnishing it with spectacular antiques and works of art from nearly three dozen countries.

The home has many remarkable features. The library, which was added by Alva Belmont, has four secret doors. The grand staircase is hand-carved, which took hundreds of European craftsmen three years to complete. Other noteworthy features include a huge Russian chandelier made with 13,000 crystal prisms. It is surrounded by eight smaller crystal chandeliers. There is an oval Versailles dining room ceiling that is hand sculptured. French Empire style columns, mirrored doors, and mirrored shutters create a spectacular effect. When open, they overlook the ocean. The most spectacular room and the most haunted room in the house is the ballroom.

Or should I say that the most haunted objects are in the ballroom. The most famous are a pair of salt chairs. No one is permitted to sit in them. Those who try are violently ejected by an unseen presence. Some have been thrown as far as seven or eight feet away. They are thrown up into the air and then propelled forward. But before they are thrown out of the chair, they say they feel like they are sitting on something—or someone. Just touching the chairs supposedly results in a strange sensation akin to getting a severe shock. Many have reported feeling queasy as soon as they are within close range of the chairs. Some feel suddenly cold as soon as they are in close proximity to the chairs. On one occasion, seventy visitors witnessed a large bolt of lightening shooting out of one of the chairs!

Salt chairs were once custom designed for royalty. Only kings were permitted to sit in them. A compartment was built in the chair that held a commodity once prized more than gold or jewels—salt! The king would present a bag of salt to esteemed visitors, such as foreign dignitaries. At that time, it was considered to be the finest gift the king could bestow. Perhaps the spirit of one of these kings is trying to protect his possession.

The entire ballroom is believed to be haunted by lingering spirits. One psychic claims there are fifteen lingering spirits in this room.

Visitors and family members have reported:

*a spooky feeling, as if being watched

*footsteps

*a disembodied male voice saying "Get out!"

*strange shadows are seen sometimes in one corner of the room

*lights mysteriously going on

*screams

The screams are believed to be connected to a suit of armor that is in the ballroom. A suit of armor has a helmet that is cracked. According to the legend, the crack occurred when a spear pierced the warrior's eye. It is believed that he died a slow, painful death. His anguished screams are heard on rare occasions.

But that's not all. There is a mirror in the music room that is haunted. People sometimes report their reflection is moving even though they are not! They describe their reflections as "vibrating." They also report that some items in the room that can be seen in the reflection of the mirror also appear to be vibrating.

The Tinneys placed a monk statue in their bedroom. The Tinneys saw a monk at the foot of their bed on occasion. Later, the statue was moved to the first floor near the ladies rest room. Some tour guides and visitors have reported seeing someone wearing a brown robe and a hood near the rest room. One tour guide saw it disappear into the rest room. She followed to let him know that he was going into the wrong bathroom, but she found no one in the rest room! After the psychic's visit, the monk statue was moved into the chapel. The psychic said that the monk had communicated his wishes to her while she was visiting. The monk entity has not been seen since the statue was moved to the chapel.

There have been sightings and paranormal activity in other parts of the house. Some believe Donald Tinney is one of the lingering spirits, unable even in death to leave his beloved home. There have been ghost investigations of the property, including SyFy's *Ghost Hunters*. In April 2009, Jason and Grant conducted a thorough investigation and captured evidence of paranormal activity, including hearing footsteps coming towards them and seeing the prints on thermal imaging.

The Tinneys did not allow the chairs to be photographed by visitors and the mansion is no longer open to the public. However, you can take a ghostly virtual tour of the castle (which includes a close up of the chairs), https://www.youtube.com/watch?v=kpTTGBiCwkQ

Tallman Bunk Bed

Location: Unknown

Origin: Unknown

Visitor Information: The house on Larabee Street is a private residence, and the bed is believed to have been destroyed or buried.

About The Haunted Object: This is perhaps the creepiest chapter of this book. It began so innocently with Alan and Deb Tallman buying a bunk bed for their kids in 1987. They found it in a thrift store, making a quick decision to buy the bargain-priced bed—or so they thought at the time.

It was February 1987 when they bought the bed, but it was a few months later by the time they got it out of the basement and set it in the kids' bedroom. As soon as the bed was moved out of storage, bad things began to happen. The children swore they saw a witch or something that resembled a witch. And they got sick and stayed ill with nagging health problems.

The radio started playing without anyone touching the power button and changing stations without any prompting. Doors opened and slammed shut that had never done so previously. Furniture moved on its own, especially chairs. A basement window was found on the basement floor—undamaged as if it had been carefully removed. A suitcase that was stored under a bed moved out into the middle of the room and then slid back under the bed as if moved by an invisible force. Alan's lunch box was jerked out of his hands by an unseen presence (they briefly struggled before Alan lost his grip) and thrown across the living room.

The Tallmans were understandably spooked by these strange incidents. They all had nightmares, sometimes waking up crying. They talked to their pastor. He came to their home and performed a blessing on it to "cleanse" it. Things did get better for a while, but then they got worse.

Alan Tallman began hearing voices. A raspy voice told him to *"Come here."* and directed him to the garage, where he found a fire blazing and what looked like two eyes in the windows. He ran back into the house to get the fire extinguisher from the kitchen. When he got back to the garage, he was shocked to find nothing. No fire. No signs that there had been a fire. Nothing unusual.

This disturbing event happened just one day after Alan challenged the evil entity to *"Please leave my children alone. If you want to fight, fight me!"*

After this incident, everyone was spooked. The kids refused to stay in their room alone, so Alan and Deb slept with their kids. One night, they watched in disbelief as a fog appeared out of nowhere in the middle of the bedroom. It turned into a glowing flare with vivid green eyes. And it spoke, issuing them a prophetic warning. The same raspy voice Alan had heard telling him to *"Come here"* said *"You're dead!"* and then it disappeared.

Enough was enough. The family left that cold winter night in 1988 and returned just long enough to pack their belongings. The house sat vacant for a long time but had many visitors.

The story of the hauntings had spread, and gawkers lined up on Larabee Street to see the house where blood oozed from the ceilings, and a hole to Hell existed in the basement. The stories and the number of gawkers grew as time passed.

Neighbors complained, and the sheriff's department frequently had to chase people away. They even had to arrest one man for trespassing. He claimed he was performing an exorcism. The deputy claimed he was drunk, incoherent, and waving a Bible. For a while, the house had to be barricaded and the street off-limits to everyone except for local traffic.

The stories eventually subsided, as things have a way of doing with the passage of time. The house was sold, and the new owners authorized a television show, *Unsolved Mysteries*, to film an episode in their house. Nothing unusual happened during the taping, and the new owners said nothing bad had happened to them since moving in.

But then again, there was no longer a haunted object in the house. Alan Tallman had seen to that. The first thing he did the day the family returned to collect their belongings was to destroy the bunk bed. When he was done with his annihilation, it was impossible to tell what the object had once been. However, another account reports the bunk bed was buried in a landfill.

The former home of the Tallmans

The Anguished Man

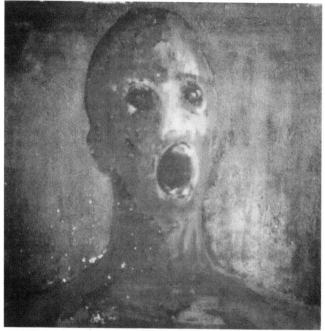

Photo by Sean Robinson, owner of this painting

Location: United Kingdom

Origin: Unknown

Visitor Information: This object is privately owned and kept in an undisclosed location. There have been many rumors about it being for sale, but that is not true.

www.anguishedman.com

About The Haunted Object: Sean Robinson should have listened to his grandmother. She told him the painting was evil and she told him why. Upon her death, however, he went up into her attic where she had hidden it for twenty-five years and claimed it.

His grandmother had reluctantly accepted the strange painting as a gift. But soon after bringing it home she began seeing a ghostly figure of a man in her home. As you can imagine, the sightings scared her. After she took the painting upstairs and hid it away in her attic, the sightings stopped.

Perhaps Sean Robinson felt her tale was just a story dreamed up by an old, senile lady. Or perhaps curiosity just got the better of him. For whatever reason, Sean put the painting in his bedroom, carefully propped up against the wall. And that's when bad things started happening to his family.

First, his son fell down the stairs. His wife felt someone stroking her head while she was trying to sleep. They heard banging noises and heard crying coming from the corner of their bedroom. The family experienced unexplainable nausea, nightmares, migraines, and nose bleeds. But the most disturbing event was the sighting of a ghostly figure at the foot of their bed. This is exactly what Sean's grandmother described happened to her! But unlike his grandmother, Sean's wife was not content for the painting to remain in their home. She insisted he remove it from their house, so the painting went into storage.

Before the painting was removed from the home, Sean Robinson set up a camera to capture some of these strange happenings on audio and video tape. He recorded doors slamming seemingly by themselves. He also picked up some orbs, a smoky haze, and the painting falling over on its own, as if it had been knocked over by some unseen presence.

The painting, known as *The Anguished Man*, clearly captures the image of an anguished or tortured soul. While the artist is unknown, testing has revealed that blood is mixed in with the oil colors.

Reportedly, the blood belonged to the artist. How creepy is that? It is also known that shortly after he finished this now famous painting, he killed himself.

Sean has contacted leading paranormal investigators in the hopes of finding some answers. One such investigation occurred on May 18, 2013 at Chillingham Castle in Northumberland. It was led by John Blackman, who is with *Mysteria Paranormal*. The painting was placed in the center of the room. A group of twenty paranormal experts was assembled around it in a séance circle. They began asking questions. Soon after that, a heavy wooden bench was knocked over by an unseen presence. Suddenly, the room grew very cold, and then a dark figure appeared next to the painting. It soon disappeared and did not respond when further questions were asked. The paranormal investigators have no clue who or what this entity is. It could be the spirit of the anguished artist who created the painting. Or it could be an evil spirit who has attached itself to this object.

There have been rumors the Robinsons are selling the painting, but Sean has publicly stated that he is not selling it. Maybe he is the best guardian of it. He will, however, continue to search for answers. You can see his latest update was posted in February 2016 on YouTube, during which he reveals that the painting (or rather the spirit connected to it) is still active:

https://www.youtube.com/watch?v=UiPT4FDztuc

THE HANDS RESIST HIM

The Hands Resist Him

Location: Unknown

Origin: 1972

Visitor Information: None

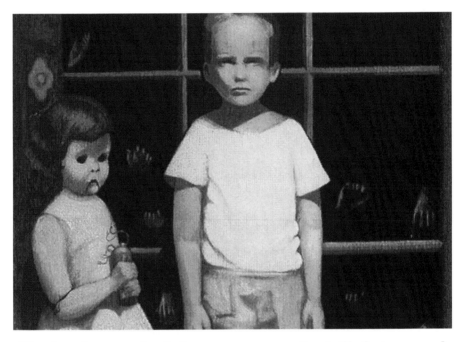

Here's a close up of painting so you can see the doll's features and the eerie handprints in the glass.

About The Haunted Object: This story begins in 1972. Artist Bill Stoneham was under contract to create two paintings each and every month for the Feingarten Gallery. But this month Stoneham was having trouble coming up with something to paint and his deadline was fast approaching.

Inspiration struck when his wife finished a poem she had been writing, "Hands Resist Him." Stoneham used a photo that had been taken more than twenty years old, when he was a child, as the basis for his painting. The photo was taken when Stoneham was five years old. He was standing on his stoop posing with a little girl from his neighborhood. For his painting, Stoneham changed the little girl to a life-sized doll and his front door became a glass-paneled portal. He added disembodied hands pressing again the other side of the door. They were meant to represent a portal between the real world and a dream world.

As if a little boy standing next to a freakishly life-life doll with the detached hands of children pressing against the glass, as if begging to be freed isn't creepy enough, this story gets grows more bizarre and scarier.

The painting was bought by actor John Marley, whose career was cemented by his role in *The Godfather*. Within three years, all three people who were closely associated with this painting were dead. This included the gallery owner who handled the painting, Charles Feingarten. Also, the *L.A. Times* art critic who wrote the only review of the painting, Henry Seldis, and the first owner of the painting, John Marley, died untimely deaths.

For many years, the painting remained lost. It had either been hidden or abandoned in an old brewery in California. But when the space was renovated, the painting was discovered, and the curse revived.

Hands Resist Him was listed for sale on eBay in 2000 by the couple who ended up with the abandoned painting. The eBay listing is sensationally scary:

"When we received this painting, we thought it was really good art. At the time we wondered a little why a seemingly perfectly find painting would be discarded like that. Today we don't! One morning our 4 ½-year-old daughter claimed that children in the picture were fighting and coming into the room during the night."

The father set up a video camera that was motion-sensitive, meaning it would begin recording if there were any activity. He planned to use the footage to show his daughter that she had nothing to be afraid of. Instead, the father was deeply disturbed to see a little boy crawl out of the painting!

Despite the grim and graphic description, the painting received thousands of views, got nearly three dozen bids, and sold for $1,025. Some folks who viewed the painting on the auction site claimed they experienced supernatural encounters just from looking at the painting. This included reports of becoming nauseous, hearing voices and feeling hot or cold for no reason.

The winning bid was Kim Smith, a gallery owner. After a few strange incidents, Smith moved the painting into storage where it remains to this day. Smith plans to sell the painting when she feels the time is right. *Buyer beware!*

Stoneham maintains there is nothing spooky, creepy, haunted, or cursed about his painting.

In a strange epilogue to this tale, an art collector commissioned two more paintings, *Resistance at the Threshold* in 2004 and *Threshold of Revelation* in 2012. The former is a painting of the boy as an old man but posing alongside with the same doll. The latter has the boy as an old man, and the doll is a real girl holding a doll's mask, and I can't tell what the old man is doing in the water. It looks like it might be a walking stick and fish.

Valentino Ring

Location: Unknown

Origin: Unknown before the 1920s when Valentino bought the ring

Visitor Information: None

About The Haunted Object: Rudolph Valentino was a huge, Hollywood star, so much so that I know the name despite him being dead many years before I was even born. He is legendary, in the company of Gary Cooper, John Barrymore, Greta Garbo, and Olivia de Havilland. In fact, Valentino was one of the greatest silent film stars of all time. His life was a charmed one—until it became a cursed one.

Valentino was born on May 6, 1895. He was the son of an Italian veterinary surgeon and his mother was a French. His first job upon immigrating to America was a dancer-for-hire in a New York City night club. He earned ten cents a dance.

It wasn't long before he was discovered. He landed his first role in 1921, *The Four Horsemen of the Apocalypse*. Women worldwide quickly took notice of this suave, sexy man with captivating eyes.

His career took off and Valentino became a star almost overnight. The A-list actor was in demand with studios, producers, and theater audiences. However, the sexy star found himself in a spot of trouble after getting involved with New York socialite, Blanca de Saulles. She suffered a scandalous divorce during which time her wealthy and influential husband had Valentino arrested on vice charges. The charges didn't stick, but Valentino didn't stick around for more charges to be drummed up.

He fled to the West Coast and began again in San Francisco. Passing a jewelry store one afternoon, he noticed an unusual ring. He was compelled to buy it. The owner agreed it was a wonderful piece of jewelry, but cautioned Valentino that it was cursed.

Not believing in such nonsense, Valentino bought the ring. He wore the ring home. And so began the curse, if you believe in such things.

The first flop of his career occurred soon after acquiring the ring. *The Young Rajah* was so bad that it nearly ruined Valentino's career. It was nearly two years before he could land another movie role. During this time, a small seed of doubt crept into Valentino's mind. What if there was such a thing as a cursed object and what if his ring was cursed?

He put the ring away and soon after that got another starring role. His career was back on track. Confident once again, Valentino dug out his beloved ring and began wearing it for "good luck" while filming *Son of Sheik*.

Suddenly, Valentino's health declined. He was often ill during the making of this movie. He pushed himself to keep going, well aware this was his shot at a comeback. After collapsing on the set one day, he could no longer ignore his condition. The diagnosis was bleeding ulcers, which required surgery.

Emergency surgery was performed, and while there is always a risk with any surgery, this surgery is considered routine and usually goes well. In this case, Valentino died a couple of days later from complications from surgery. He was just thirty-one years old.

After his death on August 26, 1926, the ring passed onto his girlfriend, Pola Negri. She immediately began wearing the ring. It made her feel closer to Valentino, which helped her cope with her grief. Soon, however, Negri grew gravely ill. Her health got so bad that she was unable to work for a long time. Recalling talk of a curse, she gave the ring to Russ Columbo.

Columbo was a singer who greatly resembled Valentino's appearance. He was honored to receive the ring and wore it with pride— right up until his death shortly after that. He died in a tragic and mysterious shooting. His case remains unsolved.

The ring passed on to Columbo's best friend, Joe Casino. Joe had heard the stories about the cursed ring. He hid it rather than risk wearing it. As time passed, Casino began to question the wisdom of doing nothing with the ring. He began thinking he should wear it and enjoy it or sell it and make some money. He decided on the former. Just a few days after he started wearing the ring, he was run over by a truck.

Joe Casino's brother, Del Casino, inherited the ring. His home was robbed one night. Among other possessions, the burglar stole the Valentino ring. Police killed him during his escape attempt. The ring was returned to Del Casino.

A movie producer approached Del Casino about borrowing the ring. He was making a movie about Valentino's life and felt the ring was an important part of his life and legend. Casino agreed to loan him the ring. The producer, Edward Small, gave the ring to the actor portraying Valentino, Jack Dunn. Just a few short days later, Dunn was dead from an extremely rare blood disease. He was barely twenty-one years old.

Casino put the ring in a bank vault for safe keeping after this latest incident. Several months later, the bank was robbed. One of the items stolen was the Valentino ring. The gang was soon apprehended. When the leader, Alfred Hahn, learned about the ring, he reportedly told authorities he would never have robbed that vault if he had known.

The location of the ring is unknown. It was returned to Casino after the trial, but what happened since then is anybody's guess. It is presumed to be locked up somewhere for safekeeping, but no one has come forward and claimed ownership.

Valentino's manager, George Ullman, arranged a public viewing of Valentino's body in New York. He thought the fans would appreciate the chance to say goodbye to their idol. His plan backfired, and he soon had to scrap his plans. Close to 100,000 women swarmed the grounds, nearly causing a riot. When Valentino's body was transported from New York to Los Angeles for burial, several despondent female fans committed suicide. Ironically, Valentino died a legend, but he was broke and $3 million in debt. There was no money in his estate for his funeral or burial. His friend, June Mathis, donated a crypt she owned at Hollywood Forever Cemetery.

FYI: His most popular films include:

Camille (1921)

The Four Horseman of the Apocalypse (1921)

The Sheik (1921)

Blood and Sand (1922)

The Eagle (1925)

Cobra (1925)

The Son of the Sheik (1925)

*Notice the gap in his movies from 1922 – 1925. This is supposedly due to the curse of the ring.

Rudolph Valentino's sultry eyes helped make him famous and a worldwide sex symbol. Thousands of women around the world mourned his death.

More Spooky Objects

Black Orlov. This is a black orlov diamond that is also known as the 'Eye of Brahma'. According to legend, it was stolen from a Hindu shrine. The stone was used as one of the eyes in a sacred Hindu statue of Brahma. The gem has had many owners and most took their own lives soon after possessing the orlov. Russian Princess Nadia Vygin-Orlov leaped to her death from a building in Rome. Princess Leonila Viktorovna-Bariatinsky also leaped to her death soon after acquiring the Black Orlov. In 1932, diamond dealer, J.W. Paris, jumped from a Manhattan skyscraper right after buying the diamond in Europe and traveling to New York in search of a buyer. The curse continued until the Eye of Brahma was sold to Charles Wilson, who had the diamond re-cut by an Austrian jeweler during the 1950s, in an attempt to end the curse. The cutting took two years to complete! Perhaps it was worth the wait as it seems to have worked. No tragedies have been documented in connection with the diamond since that time. The 124-diamond necklace was worn by actress Felicity Huffman to a Hollywood Oscars awards ceremony a few years ago.

Blarney Stone. Kissing the Blarney Stone is said to bring good luck and has become a tradition for tourists in Ireland. What is not as widely known is that anyone who tries to take a piece of the stone home as a souvenir is cursed. Many who have taken a bit of the Blarney Stone home with them end up mailing it back to castle officials with a note apologizing for their actions and pleading that their misfortunes be reversed. Visitors who have swiped a piece of the rock for posterity report they have lost their jobs, suffered financial hardships, and been stricken with health problems, including bouts of depression, shortly after returning home.

James Dean's beloved sports car, "**Little Bastard,**" is said to be cursed. On September 30, 1955, the Little Bastard was in a head-on collision that killed the *Rebel Without a Cause* actor. Reportedly, Dean showed the car to Sir Alec Guinness during a lunch meeting. Guinness surprised him with a warning, "If you get in that car, you will be dead by this time next week." His prophecy rang true. Dean was killed in a collision just a few days later while driving the Porsche. The wrecked vehicle was bought by George Barris for $2,500 for parts. A mechanic who was trying to salvage all the parts that could be salvaged was crushed when the car fell on him. The intact engine was sold to a doctor, who had it installed in his hobby race car. He was killed while driving the car soon after the Porsche engine had been put into his car. The Little Bastard's drive shaft was installed in another race car and the driver was killed instantly when the vehicle malfunctioned and flipped. A young man bought two tires from the Porsche and the first time he drove his car after installing the tires, both tires blew simultaneously, causing a near fatal crash. The wrecked car was donated to a California Highway Patrol safety exhibit. While in storage awaiting display, a mysterious fire broke out. It destroyed all the cars and other items in storage, except for the Porsche. Several strange events occurred while the car was on exhibit. That may be the reason the car is no longer on display. In fact, its whereabouts are unknown.

This is a grey 1955 Porsche Spyder known as 'Little Bastard'.

Koh-i-Noor Diamond. Koh-Noor is Persian for 'Mountain of Light'. Believed to be stolen from India during a 1310 raid, the Diamond of Babur brings violent death and anguish to any man who possesses it. Emperor Sher Shah Suri was renowned for his good luck and fortune, at least until he came into possession of this diamond. Shortly thereafter, he was killed in a freak explosion. Another owner, Jalal Khan, was murdered. Luckily, the gem has ended up in the possession of a woman, Queen Elizabeth II. It is displayed, along with many other Crown jewels, in the Tower of London. The governments of India, Pakistan, Iran and Afghanistan have claimed ownership of the Koh-i-Noor, but to no avail. The British monarchy insists the gem was obtained legally under the terms of the Treaty of Lahore.

Uluru Rocks. This is a giant rock formation in the Australian outback. Just like with the Blarney Stone, tourists sometimes take a piece of Uluru home with them, even though it is illegal to do so. Because this is sacred Aboriginal grounds, it is believed they have placed a curse to any and all who try to remove Uluru from its sacred spot. Those who have taken a bit of Uluru home with them claim to have all kinds of bad things happen to them soon after arriving home.

Dear Reader,

Thank you for your interest in *Spookiest Objects!* I spent a great deal of time compiling this information into what I believe is an easy-to-read, useful reference. I would love to hear from you if you'd like to post a question or comment about this book or share a ghost story www.terrancezepke.com. I do respond to all comments. If you'd like to get lots of travel tips be sure to sign up for my *Terrance Talks Travel* blog on www.terrancetalkstravel.com, which will also alert you when the latest episodes of my travel show are available and reveal my weekly TRIP PICK.

I would also like to ask you to please share your feedback about this book on Amazon or your favorite bookseller so that other readers might discover this title too.

Authors appreciate readers more than you realize and we dearly love and depend upon good reviews! If you've never posted a review before it is easy to do, just go to your favorite online bookseller and tell folks what you liked about this book and why you (hopefully) recommend it.

Terrance

TERRANCE ZEPKE
Series Reading Order
& Guide

Series List

Most Haunted Series

Terrance Talks Travel Series

Cheap Travel Series

Spookiest Series

Stop Talking Series

Carolinas for Kids Series

Ghosts of the Carolinas Series

Books & Guides for the Carolinas Series

& More Books by Terrance Zepke

≈

Introduction

Here is a list of titles by Terrance Zepke. They are presented in chronological order although they do not need to be read in any particular order.

Also included is an author bio, a personal message from Terrance, and some other information you may find helpful.

All books are available as eBooks and print books. They can be found on Amazon, Barnes and Noble, Kobo, Apple iBooks, Smashwords, or through your favorite independent bookseller.

For more about this author and her books visit her Author Page at:

http://www.amazon.com/Terrance-Zepke/e/B000APJNIA/.

You can also connect with Terrance on Twitter **@terrancezepke** or on

www.facebook.com/terrancezepke

www.pinterest.com/terrancezepke

www.goodreads.com/terrancezepke

Sign up for weekly email notifications of the *Terrance Talks Travel* blog to be the first to learn about new episodes of her travel show, travel tips, free downloadable TRAVEL REPORTS, and discover her TRIP PICK OF THE WEEK at www.terrancetalkstravel.com or sign up for her *Mostly Ghostly* blog at www.terrancezepke.com.

≈

You can follow her travel show, **TERRANCE TALKS TRAVEL: ÜBER ADVENTURES on** www.blogtalkradio.com/terrancetalkstravel or subscribe to it at **iTunes.**

Warning: Listening to this show could lead to a spectacular South African safari, hot-air ballooning over the Swiss Alps, Disney Adventures, and Tornado Tours!

≈

Terrance Zepke is co-host of the writing show, **A WRITER'S JOURNEY: FROM BLANK PAGE TO PUBLISHED.** All episodes can be found on **iTunes** or on <u>www.terrancezepke.com</u>.

≈

AUTHOR BIO

Terrance Zepke studied Journalism at the University of Tennessee and later received a Master's degree in Mass Communications from the University of South Carolina. She studied parapsychology at the renowned Rhine Research Center.

Zepke spends much of her time happily traveling around the world but always returns home to the Carolinas where she lives part-time in both states. She has written hundreds of articles and close to three dozen books. She is the host of *Terrance Talks Travel: Über Adventures* and co-host of *A Writer's Journey: From Blank Page to Published*. Additionally, this award-winning and best-selling author has been featured in many publications and programs, such as NPR, CNN, The Washington Post, Associated Press, Travel with Rick Steves, Around the World, Publishers Weekly, World Travel & Dining with Pierre Wolfe, Good Morning Show, The Learning Channel, and The Travel Channel.

When she's not investigating haunted places, searching for pirate treasure, or climbing lighthouses, she is most likely packing for her next adventure to some far flung place, such as Reykjavik or Kwazulu Natal. Some of her favorite adventures include piranha fishing on the Amazon, shark cage diving in South Africa, hiking the Andes Mountains Inca Trail, camping in the Himalayas, dog-sledding in the Arctic Circle, and a gorilla safari in the Congo.

≈

MOST HAUNTED SERIES

A Ghost Hunter's Guide to the Most Haunted Places in America (2012)
https://read.amazon.com/kp/embed?asin=B0085SG22O&preview=newt
ab&linkCode=kpe&ref_=cm_sw_r_kb_dp_zerQwb1AMJ0R4

A Ghost Hunter's Guide to the Most Haunted Houses in America (2013)
https://read.amazon.com/kp/embed?asin=B00C3PUMGC&preview=ne
wtab&linkCode=kpe&ref_=cm_sw_r_kb_dp_BfrQwb1WF1Y6T

A Ghost Hunter's Guide to the Most Haunted Hotels & Inns in America
(2014)
https://read.amazon.com/kp/embed?asin=B00C3PUMGC&preview=ne
wtab&linkCode=kpe

A Ghost Hunter's Guide to the Most Haunted Historic Sites in America
(2016)
https://read.amazon.com/kp/embed?asin=B01LXADK90&preview=new
tab&linkCode=kpe&ref_=cm_sw_r_kb_dp_RzU2yb64YCC1Q

*The Ghost Hunter's MOST HAUNTED Box Set (3 in 1): Discover
America's Most Haunted Destinations* (2016)
https://read.amazon.com/kp/embed?asin=B01HISAAJM&preview=newt
ab&linkCode=kpe&ref_=cm_sw_r_kb_dp_ulz-xbNKND7VT

**MOST HAUNTED and SPOOKIEST Sampler Box Set: Featuring *A GHOST
HUNTER'S GUIDE TO THE MOST HAUNTED PLACES IN AMERICA* and
SPOOKIEST CEMETERIES (2017)**

https://read.amazon.com/kp/embed?asin=B01N17EEOM&preview=ne
wtab&linkCode=kpe&ref_=cm_sw_r_kb_dp_.JFLybCTN3QEF

≈

TERRANCE TALKS TRAVEL SERIES

Terrance Talks Travel: A Pocket Guide to South Africa (2015)
https://read.amazon.com/kp/embed?asin=B00PSTFTLI&preview=newta
b&linkCode=kpe&ref_=cm_sw_r_kb_dp_pirQwb12XZX65

Terrance Talks Travel: A Pocket Guide to African Safaris (2015)
https://read.amazon.com/kp/embed?asin=B00PSTFZSA&preview=newt
ab&linkCode=kpe&ref_=cm_sw_r_kb_dp_jhrQwb0P8Z87G

Terrance Talks Travel: A Pocket Guide to Adventure Travel (2015)
https://read.amazon.com/kp/embed?asin=B00UKMAVQG&preview=ne
wtab&linkCode=kpe&ref_=cm_sw_r_kb_dp_ThrQwb1PVVZAZ

*Terrance Talks Travel: A Pocket Guide to Florida Keys (including Key
West & The Everglades)* (2016)
https://read.amazon.com/kp/embed?asin=B01EWHML58&preview=ne
wtab&linkCode=kpe&ref_=cm_sw_r_kb_dp_kuU2ybQJCECXQ

Terrance Talks Travel: The Quirky Tourist Guide to Key West (2017)
https://read.amazon.com/kp/embed?asin=B01N3BF80O&preview=newt
ab&linkCode=kpe&ref_=cm_sw_r_kb_dp_gqU2yb4ZNW7NT

Terrance Talks Travel: The Quirky Tourist Guide to Cape Town (2017)
https://read.amazon.com/kp/embed?asin=B01N6YKI77&preview=newt
ab&linkCode=kpe&ref_=cm_sw_r_kb_dp_jsU2yb6H1KR5Q

Terrance Talks Travel: The Quirky Tourist Guide to Reykjavik (2017)
https://read.amazon.com/kp/embed?asin=B06XJZZCN5&preview=newt
ab&linkCode=kpe&ref_=cm_sw_r_kb_dp_LpU2yb2HMFJXY

*Terrance Talks Travel: The Quirky Tourist Guide to Charleston, South
Carolina* (2017)
https://read.amazon.com/kp/embed?asin=B06XVFTBRX&preview=new
tab&linkCode=kpe&ref_=cm_sw_r_kb_dp_rnU2ybAXCTRGW

Terrance Talks Travel: The Quirky Tourist Guide to Ushuaia (2017)
https://read.amazon.com/kp/embed?asin=B06XVKNH6R&preview=ne
wtab&linkCode=kpe&ref_=cm_sw_r_kb_dp_apU2ybTFZAWK3

Terrance Talks Travel: The Quirky Tourist Guide to Antarctica (2017)
https://read.amazon.com/kp/embed?asin=B06XWG1CFH&preview=ne
wtab&linkCode=kpe&ref_=cm_sw_r_kb_dp_YnU2ybCFPF92A

African Safari Box Set: Featuring TERRANCE TALKS TRAVEL: *A Pocket Guide to South Africa* and *TERRANCE TALKS TRAVEL: A Pocket Guide to African Safaris* (2017)
https://read.amazon.com/kp/embed?asin=B01MUH6VJU&preview=ne
wtab&linkCode=kpe&ref_=cm_sw_r_kb_dp_xLFLybAQKFA0B

≈

CHEAP TRAVEL SERIES

How to Cruise Cheap! (2017)

https://read.amazon.com/kp/embed?asin=B01N6NYM1N&preview=ne
wtab&linkCode=kpe&ref_=cm_sw_r_kb_dp_YAU2ybHX177B8

How to Fly Cheap! (2017)

https://read.amazon.com/kp/embed?asin=B01N7Q81YG&preview=ne
wtab&linkCode=kpe&ref_=cm_sw_r_kb_dp_pBU2ybQ5RT43J

How to Travel Cheap! (2017)

https://read.amazon.com/kp/embed?asin=B01N7Q81YG&preview=ne
wtab&linkCode=kpe&ref_=cm_sw_r_kb_dp_j78KybJVSCXDX

How to Travel FREE or Get Paid to Travel! (2017)

https://read.amazon.com/kp/embed?asin=B01N7Q81YG&preview=ne
wtab&linkCode=kpe&ref_=cm_sw_r_kb_dp_j78KybJVSCXDX

SPOOKIEST SERIES

Spookiest Lighthouses (2013)
https://read.amazon.com/kp/embed?asin=B00EAAQA2S&preview

Spookiest Battlefields (2015)
https://read.amazon.com/kp/embed?asin=B00XUSWS3G&preview=ne
wtab&linkCode=kpe&ref_=cm_sw_r_kb_dp_okrQwb0TR9F8M

Spookiest Cemeteries (2016)
https://read.amazon.com/kp/embed?asin=B01D0FP498&preview=newta
b&linkCode=kpe&ref_=cm_sw_r_kb_dp_mCU2yb3R68RGM

*Spookiest Box Set (3 in 1): Discover America's Most Haunted
Destinations* (2016)
https://read.amazon.com/kp/embed?asin=B01HH2OM4I&preview=newt
ab&linkCode=kpe&ref_=cm_sw_r_kb_dp_Anz-xbT3SDEZS

Spookiest Objects (2017)
https://www.amazon.com/Terrance-
Zepke/e/B000APJNIA/ref=bseries_auth_1_0985539852_1

≈

STOP TALKING SERIES

Stop Talking & Start Writing Your Book (2015)
https://read.amazon.com/kp/embed?asin=B012YHTIAY&preview=newt
ab&linkCode=kpe&ref_=cm_sw_r_kb_dp_qlrQwb1N7G3YF

Stop Talking & Start Publishing Your Book (2015)
https://read.amazon.com/kp/embed?asin=B013HHV1LE&preview=newt
ab&linkCode=kpe&ref_=cm_sw_r_kb_dp_WlrQwb1F63MFD

Stop Talking & Start Selling Your Book (2015)
https://read.amazon.com/kp/embed?asin=B015YAO33K&preview=newt
ab&linkCode=kpe&ref_=cm_sw_r_kb_dp_ZkrQwb188J8BE

Stop Talking & Start Writing Your Book Series (3 in 1) Box Set (2016)
https://read.amazon.com/kp/embed?asin=B01M58J5AZ&preview=newt
ab&linkCode=kpe&ref_=cm_sw_r_kb_dp_JDU2ybNEJHGKA

≈

CAROLINAS FOR KIDS SERIES

Lighthouses of the Carolinas for Kids (2009)
http://www.amazon.com/Lighthouses-Carolinas-Kids-Terrance-
Zepke/dp/1561644293/ref=asap_bc?ie=UTF8

Pirates of the Carolinas for Kids (2009)
https://read.amazon.com/kp/embed?asin=B01BJ3VSWK&preview=new
tab&linkCode=kpe&ref_=cm_sw_r_kb_dp_rGrXwb0XDTSTA

Ghosts of the Carolinas for Kids (2011)
https://read.amazon.com/kp/embed?asin=B01BJ3VSVQ&preview=newt
ab&linkCode=kpe&ref_=cm_sw_r_kb_dp_XLrXwb0E7N1AK

≈

GHOSTS OF THE CAROLINAS SERIES

Ghosts of the Carolina Coasts (1999)
http://www.amazon.com/Ghosts-Carolina-Coasts-Terrance-
Zepke/dp/1561641758/ref=asap_bc?ie=UTF8

The Best Ghost Tales of South Carolina (2004)
http://www.amazon.com/Best-Ghost-Tales-South-
Carolina/dp/1561643068/ref=asap_bc?ie=UTF8

Ghosts & Legends of the Carolina Coasts (2005)
https://read.amazon.com/kp/embed?asin=B01AGQJABW&preview=ne
wtab&linkCode=kpe&ref_=cm_sw_r_kb_dp_VKrXwb1Q09794

The Best Ghost Tales of North Carolina (2006)
https://read.amazon.com/kp/embed?asin=B01BJ3VSV6&preview=newt
ab&linkCode=kpe&ref_=cm_sw_r_kb_dp_6IrXwb0XKT90Q

≈

BOOKS & GUIDES FOR THE CAROLINAS SERIES

Pirates of the Carolinas (2005)
http://www.amazon.com/Pirates-Carolinas-Terrance-Zepke/dp/1561643440/ref=asap_bc?ie=UTF8

Coastal South Carolina: Welcome to the Lowcountry (2006)
http://www.amazon.com/Coastal-South-Carolina-Welcome-Lowcountry/dp/1561643483/ref=asap_bc?ie=UTF8

Coastal North Carolina: Its Enchanting Islands, Towns & Communities (2011)
http://www.amazon.com/Coastal-North-Carolina-Terrance-Zepke/dp/1561645117/ref=asap_bc?ie=UTF8

Lighthouses of the Carolinas: A Short History & Guide (2011)
https://read.amazon.com/kp/embed?asin=B01AGQJA7G&preview=new tab&linkCode=kpe&ref_=cm_sw_r_kb_dp_UHrXwb09A22P1

≈

MORE BOOKS BY TERRANCE ZEPKE

Lowcountry Voodoo: Tales, Spells & Boo Hags (2009)
https://read.amazon.com/kp/embed?asin=B018WAGUC6&preview=ne
wtab&linkCode=kpe&ref_=cm_sw_r_kb_dp_UmrQwb19AVSYG

*The Encyclopedia of Cheap Travel: Save Up to 90% on Lodging,
Flights, Tours, Cruises & More!* (2011)
https://read.amazon.com/kp/embed?asin=B005WKGNKY&preview=ne
wtab&linkCode=kpe&ref_=cm_sw_r_kb_dp_InrQwb18QTWGS

Ghosts of Savannah (2012)
http://www.amazon.com/Ghosts-Savannah-Terrance-
Zepke/dp/1561645303/ref=asap_bc?ie=UTF8

How to Train Any Puppy or Dog Using Three Simple Strategies (2017)
https://read.amazon.com/kp/embed?asin=B01MZ5GN2M&preview=ne
wtab&linkCode=kpe&ref_=cm_sw_r_kb_dp_EEU2ybKVBVZC5

*Fiction books written under a pseudonym

≈

Message from the Author

The primary purpose of this guide is to introduce you to some titles you may not have known about. Another reason for it is to let you know all the ways you can connect with me. Authors love to hear from readers. We truly appreciate you more than you'll ever know. Please feel free to send me a comment or question via the comment form found on every page on www.terrancezepke.com and www.terrancetalkstravel.com or follow me on your favorite social media. Don't forget that you can also listen to my writing podcast on iTunes, **A Writer's Journey**, or my travel show, **Terrance Talks Travel: Über Adventures** on Blog Talk Radio and iTunes. The best way to make sure you don't miss any episodes of these shows (and find a complete archive of shows), new book releases and giveaways, contests, my TRIP PICK OF THE WEEK, cheap travel tips, free downloadable travel reports, and more is to subscribe to *Terrance Talks Travel* on www.terrancetalkstravel.com or *Mostly Ghostly* on www.terrancezepke.com. If you'd like to learn more about any of my books, you can find in-depth descriptions and "look inside" options through most online booksellers. Also, please note that links to book previews have been included in SERIES section of this booklet for your convenience.

Thank you for your interest and HAPPY READING!

Terrance

See the next page for a special preview of the first book in Terrance Zepke's 'MOST HAUNTED' series:

A GHOST HUNTER'S GUIDE TO THE MOST HAUNTED PLACES IN AMERICA is available in digital and print editions.

Shanghai Tunnels

FUN FACTS:

Portland has many nicknames, such as "Shanghai Capital of the World," "Worst Port in the World," "City of Roses," "Forbidden City," and "Unheavenly City." Most are related to its history of shanghaiing.

Men could go out for a few drinks and wake up at sea if they drank at the wrong place! Women were also abducted and forced into prostitution.

The tunnels are open to the public and visitors can choose from a variety of tour options, such as the "Shanghai Tunnel Ethnic History Tour" and "Shanghai Tunnel Ghost Tour."

The History

Merchants dug a network of tunnels under the city to transport merchandise to the water because it was easier than using the muddy, crowded streets to get the items to waiting ships. The tunnels also became a perfect way to handle human trafficking or shanghaiing.

Shanghaiing was an illegal activity but one that was widespread. It happened in Oregon and all over the world. Part of the problem is that local authorities and law enforcement denied its existence, tending to pretend it was not a problem.

By the mid-1800s, maritime trade was booming and there were not enough men for the crews, especially due to the Gold Rush. Ships from all over came to town and spent money while "shopping" for sailors. Also, it cut down on the transient and undesirable population. And shanghaiing served to fill a real need so perhaps they thought they were doing their civic duty!

Captains were always short-handed and resorted to some disturbing practices to find able-bodied men. They hired men, known as "shanghaiers" to help them get good men. This was accomplished going to waterfront taverns where there was lots of drinking and commotion. During the course of the night, men were plied with drinks and a good meal that might be doped with a sleep aid. When the men fell asleep or passed out, they were taken to holding cells.

Once the shanghaiers were paid the fees, they turned the men over to the captains. They were then transported to waiting ships through a series of tunnels that extended across a city (and under key buildings and businesses) down to the waterfront.

For approximately one hundred years, shanghaiing happened in waterfront towns all over the world. Among the places with the highest incidents was Portland, Oregon. It is believed that more than 2,000 people were shanghaied here during 1850 – 1940. Some put the figure much higher. Regardless of the exact number, it is obvious why Portland has been nicknamed "The Shanghai Capital of the World."

Sailors, loggers, farmers, gypsies, ranchers, cowboys, pirates, transients, and any other healthy male who frequented establishments with tunnel access underneath, such as Snug Harbor Saloon, Valhalla Saloon, Lazlo's Saloon, and Erickson's Saloon were likely to wake up somewhere far away. Reportedly, it took two full voyages or six years, for these men to get back home to Portland. Most of the ships were headed far away—to Shanghai, China. This is how the practice came to be called "shanghaiing."

A remarkably sophisticated system of tunnels snaked their way across the city from the North End (Old Town and Chinatown) to the South End (downtown). The tunnels, known now as the Portland Underground, were built under places that were likely to draw men, such as saloons, brothels, gambling parlors, and opium dens. Transients, such as cowboys, sheep herders, and migrant farmers were ideal victims. After they had been plied with so much alcohol as to be drunk enough not to put up a fight (or given knock out drops), they were lured away to well-placed trap doors.

Men waited in the tunnel under the trap door for the men and women to be dropped. They caught the drunk or drugged bodies and dragged them to holding cells to await their fate. Their shoes were taken to impede escape and broken glass was reportedly scattered through the tunnels in case they came to and managed to escape their holding cells. Just before a ship's departure, the victim was again given knock out drops and carried to the waiting vessel. By the time the victim woke up, he would be far away.

During archaeological digs, old shoes have been found in the tunnels, substantiating the stories about the removed shoes.

The Hauntings

It's no wonder these 6' x 6' holding cells and tunnels are haunted what with so much misery and tragedy. And it wasn't just men. Women were often abducted and forced into prostitution. If they refused, they were murdered. Men and women were drugged and carried out secret basement doors to the holding cells and tunnels. However, some never made it any farther. Some died as a result of the fall of being thrown or dropped through the secret trap doors.

One spirit that haunts these tunnels is believed to a woman who died when deposited into a holding cell. Today, the business is a pizzeria but back when it was a shanghai hotspot; Nina was hustling business one night when she was drugged and thrown down into the holding cell. She hit her head and suffered internal injuries that resulted in her death. Ever since that time, her spirit haunts this place. She has been seen, her perfume smelled, and she has been known to tug on the clothing of tour participants.

But Nina is not the only ghost in these tunnels. There are believed to be several spirits unhappily trapped here. Their presence is shown in many ways, such as faint whispers, moans, cries, strange lights and shapes that appear in photos, and the smell of alcohol and cologne.

Tour operators installed thirteen sets of wind chimes in the tunnels. They call them "spirit chimes." Whenever they swing or ring, that means the spirits are nearby because there is no air flow to trigger the chimes. There were a few prostitution rooms in the tunnel. A sheet hung like a curtain covered a small bed. There were rooms above the saloon that were also used for prostitution, but those were 'willing participants'. The shanghaied women were kept in the tunnels or sold into slavery.

Ghost groups have detected paranormal activity using EVPs, thermal imaging, and shadow detectors, which show unexplainable light shadowy mist. Some visitors to the tunnels report feeling lightheaded, dizzy and/or queasy feeling. Unexplained footsteps are heard and the sounds of old doors "creaking" open.

Visitor Information

Tours are offered by the non-profit group, Cascade Geographic Society. They last ninety minutes and explain the history and haunting of these tunnels. I've seen some unfavorable reviews online by participants who say they saw only a small brick room or holding cell under a business. I believe they are mistaking this experience given by a local business with the full tour provided by Cascade Geographic Society.

The tour starts above ground at Hobo's Restaurant at 120 N.W. Third Avenue. Hobo's was formerly Lazlo's Saloon and one of several sites renowned for shanghaiing. The restaurant does not take reservations or give tours. For more information, visit www.cgsstore.tripod.com, www.shanghaitunnels.info

Portland is 3 hours (173 miles) from Seattle, Washington and 15 hours (962 miles) from Los Angeles, California.

Sample books from both popular series for one low price!

Click this link to see a free preview:
https://read.amazon.com/kp/embed?asin=B01N17EEOM&preview=new
tab&linkCode=kpe&ref_=cm_sw_r_kb_dp_hge8yb4H9HBBA

Index

Made in the USA
Middletown, DE
21 September 2019